D0585210

TRUE
DUBLIN

TRUE DUBLIN

C. J. McCanney

MERCIER PRESS
Irish Publisher - Irish Story

MERCIER PRESS

Cork

www.mercierpress.ie

© C. J. McCanney, 2015

© Images: see captions for copyright holders

ISBN: 978 1 78117 243 8

10 9 8 7 6 5 4 3 2 1

A CIP record for this title is available from the British Library

Printed and bound in the EU.

CONTENTS

Bank of Ireland cheque. This picture didn't strictly fit into any of my chapters, but it was far too interesting to leave out. An image of a cheque from 1847, it serves to illustrate that while the Great Famine was devastating Ireland's rural poor, the situation in Dublin was a bit more complex. In 1847 £130 was a vast sum of money, but transactions such as this were a routine occurrence at this institution. Then, as now, vast wealth existed alongside abject poverty in Dublin.
(*Courtesy of the Ken Finlay Collection*)

INTRODUCTION

In the 1870s Dublin was an integral city of the United Kingdom and the British Empire and, the abortive Fenian Rising of 1867 notwithstanding, seemed copper-fastened into this arrangement. In some respects it was a city that today's residents would barely recognise. The telephone was still a novelty, with only a handful of subscribers in the whole of Dublin by the 1880s. Similarly, motor cars, insofar as they existed, were playthings of rich eccentrics, rarely seen on the streets of Dublin. Cinema, radio and powered flight were all still pipe dreams. The GAA did not yet exist. Croke Park was still known as the City and Suburban Racecourse and would continue to be for many years to come.

However, newly conceived technologies were beginning to sweep aside centuries-old practices and a new political and social order was taking form, a process that would be sped up by the violence of the new century. An influx from the country-side, spurred by the Great Famine, was underway, and as the population rose the suburbs of Dublin began to take shape away from the historical city core, although Dublin still contained a plethora of villages primarily rural in aspect. The First Home Rule Bill, rejected by Westminster in 1886, was indicative of a renewed desire for self-government and was only one way in which nationalist Ireland asserted itself during the period. At the same time primarily Dublin-based intellectuals and artists were spearheading a cultural reawakening. The 1880s and 1890s saw the creation of the Gaelic League, the creation of the GAA and the codification of its games. It also saw a literary blossoming of works in English that drew heavily on Irish myth and history for inspiration.

In the decades following 1900, Dublin underwent an immense change, at a rate perhaps never seen before or indeed since. By the mid-1920s, it formed the capital of the nascent twenty-six county Irish Free State, which slowly but inexorably removed its remaining political ties with the United Kingdom. At the same time the new technologies that were only beginning to be used just a few decades earlier, were becoming increasingly everyday parts of Dubliners' lives, as were dozens of other innovations.

These decades still hold a fascination for Dubliners and people from farther afield.

This is in no small part, I imagine, thanks to the enduring international popularity of James Joyce's masterwork, *Ulysses*, set in Dublin on an ordinary day in June 1904. In a broader sense, the fashions of late Victorian and Edwardian society also have a lasting appeal. Similarly the events of Easter Week 1916, concentrated in Dublin and its environs, and subsequent events during the War of Independence and Civil War formed potent foundation myths for the nascent state, which continue to resonate with Irish people today.

What makes this era ripe for a visual history is the simple fact that photography had taken off in a big way. While various photographic methods had been invented some years previously, it wasn't until the 1880s, in the wake of perfection of the dry plate photography process, that Irish towns and cities were photographed systematically by commercial agencies. Images of Ireland and Irish people before the 1880s do exist, and indeed several are included in this collection, but they're dwarfed in number by the vast output of the agencies in subsequent years. Amateur photography also became popular during the same period.

The images in this book are drawn from a number of sources, including the Lawrence Collection, the Eason Collection and the Clarke Collection, which are housed at the National Library of Ireland. The National Library has a vast hoard of photographs from the era, providing a priceless visual record of Irish life during those years. Other images include postcards produced by Valentine & Sons and other postcard firms, which were acquired from the Fingal Local Studies Collection as well as from Ken Finlay, a historian and collector, without whose help this book would not have been possible. Still other photographs were acquired from the US Library of Congress, which houses Photochrom images from around Ireland taken in the 1890s and produced by a firm in Detroit, Michigan. A number of the images in this book are taken from publications such as *The Lepracaun* magazine. Images and information were also provided by Bob Montgomery, Swords Museum, Malahide Historical Society and a number of other private individuals.

Through these photographs, postcards and the other visual artefacts, we are afforded glimpses into the myriad ways in which Dubliners, rich and poor, rural and urban, lived their lives during those tumultuous decades. The images in this book are divided into a number of broad thematic categories, but remember, every image tells its own story!

THE CITY'S STREETS

O'Connell Street in Dublin is probably one of the most recognisable streets in Europe, so it seemed fitting to start this collection with a view of some of the city's streets. Not all of these are as grand as O'Connell Street, but they all reflect the busy life of the city and how much it has changed, yet is still recognisable in these images to the true Dubliner.

Sackville Street from Carlisle Bridge, between 1860 and 1864. This photograph shows what was at this time known as the Carlisle Bridge and the bottom of Sackville Street. Note that the bridge is quite a lot narrower than the street itself and there is no sign of the signature statues that today line the middle of what is now O'Connell Street. A horse trough sits roughly where the statue of Daniel O'Connell was constructed between 1864 and 1882. Construction of the modern O'Connell Bridge began in 1877. This photograph was likely a long exposure given the technological limitations of the day.

Overleaf: **Sackville Street, c. 1901.** Just a few decades later the same scene h[...] altered irrevocably. In the foreground stands the statue of William Smith O'Bri[...] which later migrated to O'Connell Street. O'Connell has taken his place on the stre[...] as has Sir John Gray (erected in 1879) and the bridge now matches the street width. The pyramid-like roof of the Dublin Bread Company's brand-new buildi[...] can be seen jutting up on the right-hand side of the street. Sadly this building last[...] little more than fifteen years, as it was destroyed during the Easter Rising. *(Courtesy of the Library of Congress, LC-DIG-ppmsc-09876)*

12102. - SACKVILLE STREET & O'CONNELL BRIDGE, DUBLI

Looking towards Eden Quay, *c.* 1890s. The Custom House is an undeniably splendid building and Dubliners are justly proud of it. However, due to modern development it feels a bit out of reach from the main thoroughfares of the city, a bit aloof. From this vantage point, at a time before that development cluttered the view, the building seems welcomed back into the fold.
(*Courtesy of the National Library of Ireland*)

EDEN QUAY, DUBLIN. 2267 W. L.

North Earl Street, c. 1900. This picture just oozes prosperity. It looks as if, amid the throng, you could have all your earthly desires fulfilled. The street had tea shops, sweet shops, shoe shops, clothes shops, pipe and tobacco dealers, bookshops, newsagents and shops selling sewing machines, among other things. Yet amid all this wealth, this consumption, at the front of the crowd stands a boy with no shoes. North Earl Street, like many of the streets surrounding Sackville Street, sustained extensive damage in the Easter Rising.

(*Courtesy of the National Library of Ireland*)

Cook Street, corner of Lower Bridge Street looking towards Wormwood Gate, 1888. A contrast to the prosperity of North Earl Street can be clearly seen in this photograph taken by James Talbot Power, a Power's Whiskey heir. In the late nineteenth and early twentieth centuries tens of thousands of Dubliners lived in squalid, overcrowded conditions. This image shows the narrow tenement-laden streets near Christchurch Cathedral, where thousands of the poorest Dubliners lived at the time. Due to slum clearances in the early twentieth century and subsequent development, the landscape of this area has changed immensely in the intervening years, but it is interesting to consider what life must have been like for the onlookers captured here. One can only hope that, for the youngest at least, the future was brighter.
(*Courtesy of the National Library of Ireland*)

Tenements, Poole Street and Michael's Lane (*overleaf*), *c.* 1890s. Shortly after these photographs were taken, the buildings on Michael's Lane were replaced with better housing, but there were still slums throughout the city. *The Report on Dublin Housing*, 1914, suggested remedies for the housing situation, but, despite incremental improvements, there were still some Dubliners living in tenement conditions as late as the 1960s. (*Courtesy of the National Library of Ireland*)

POOLE ST. DUBLIN. 7880. W L.

MICHAEL'S LANE. DUBLIN. 8895. W. L

Lady on Sackville Street, *c.* 1902. In contrast to the figures in the last two images is this elegant lady, photographed by J. J. Clarke, passing the Cathal Ua Broin newsagents near the corner of what are now Parnell Street and O'Connell Street. Meanwhile the young boys congregated in the background appear to be up to mischief of some kind. The newsagent's shop sign being in Irish is a clear sign of the impact that the Gaelic League was having in the city at the time.

(*Courtesy of the National Library of Ireland*)

Two ladies walking down Grafton Street, *c.* 1903. These two ladies passing 51 Grafton Street were also snapped by Clarke, who left a small but fantastic collection of photographs of Ireland from around 1900. Unlike a lot of photos from that era, his are not staid or posed. The lady on the left seems to have pioneered a move that would later become popular with celebrities and convicted criminals alike, as they try to avoid the gaze of the press.

(*Courtesy of the National Library of Ireland*)

South Great Georges Street, Dublin

WESTMORELAND STREET, DUBLIN.

Opposite top: **South Great George's Street, *c*. 1905.** Then, as now, South Great George's Street was a bustling shopping and entertainment area as well as a major artery through the city to the south-western suburbs. George's Street Arcade, then known as the South City Markets, can be seen in the background. This building sustained extensive damage from a fire in August 1892, but was restored and remains a popular market to this day.
(*Courtesy of the Ken Finlay Collection*)

Opposite bottom: **Westmoreland Street, *c*. 1910.** This postcard, issued by Valentine & Sons, affords a view of Westmoreland Street, facing away from the river towards Trinity College and the Bank of Ireland. A banner across Westmoreland Street advertises the *Evening Telegraph*, which was Dublin's leading evening paper for most of its existence, until it folded in 1924. One of the most famous fictional Dubliners, Leopold Bloom, sells advertising for the paper in the book *Ulysses*.
(*Courtesy of the Ken Finlay Collection*)

Below: **Lower Sackville Street, *c*. 1910.** The arrows indicate the location of the Waverley Hotel. It, along with several nearby buildings, was obliterated during the fighting of Easter Week, 1916.
(*Courtesy of the Ken Finlay Collection*)

Upper Sackville Street, looking towards Nelson's Pillar, *c.* 1903–08. This photograph appears to have been taken from upstairs in the Rotunda Hospital. The Conradh Na Gaeilge (Gaelic League) premises two doors up from the Gresham Hotel is another reminder of how popular the Gaelic revival was in the city at the

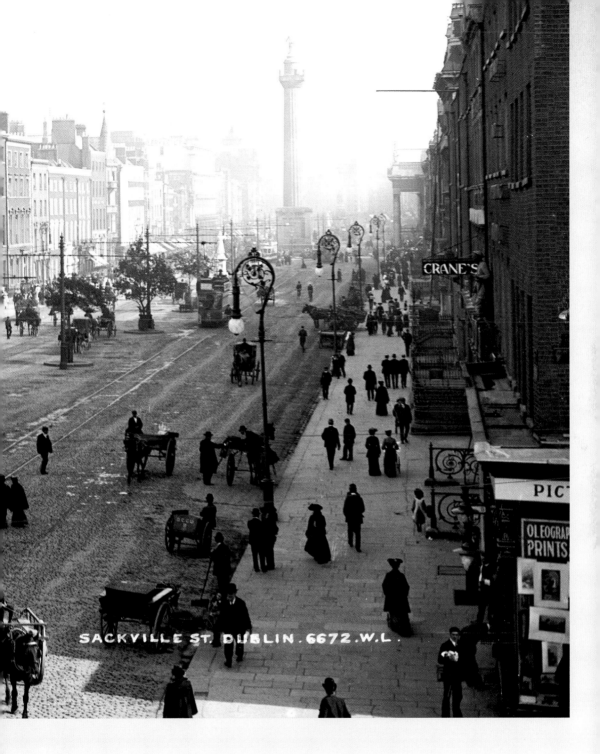

SACKVILLE ST. DUBLIN. 6672. W.L.

time. Although motor cars were becoming more popular, it's worth noting that a photograph like this could still be taken, devoid of any. The striped hut that appears on the left was the cabmen's shelter.

(*Courtesy of the National Library of Ireland*)

Hardwicke Street from North Frederick Street, 1912. The view of St George's church on Hardwicke Place from North Frederick Street is one of the iconic vistas of Dublin city. Even today, with the buildings on either side of Hardwicke Street largely replaced by more modern dwellings, it still presents a striking scene. Bicycle theft must not have been as major a concern in Dublin in those days as it was to become later, judging by the bikes simply propped up along the kerb. The sharp-eyed

viewer will also notice the sign outside the newsagent to the right asking 'Which Town Has The Prettiest Girls?' Sadly we don't know the answer. The Boons and Blessings advertisement is for Macniven & Cameron Ltd of Edinburgh, a printing and stationary company best known for their three types of pen nibs shown here. (*Courtesy of the National Library of Ireland*)

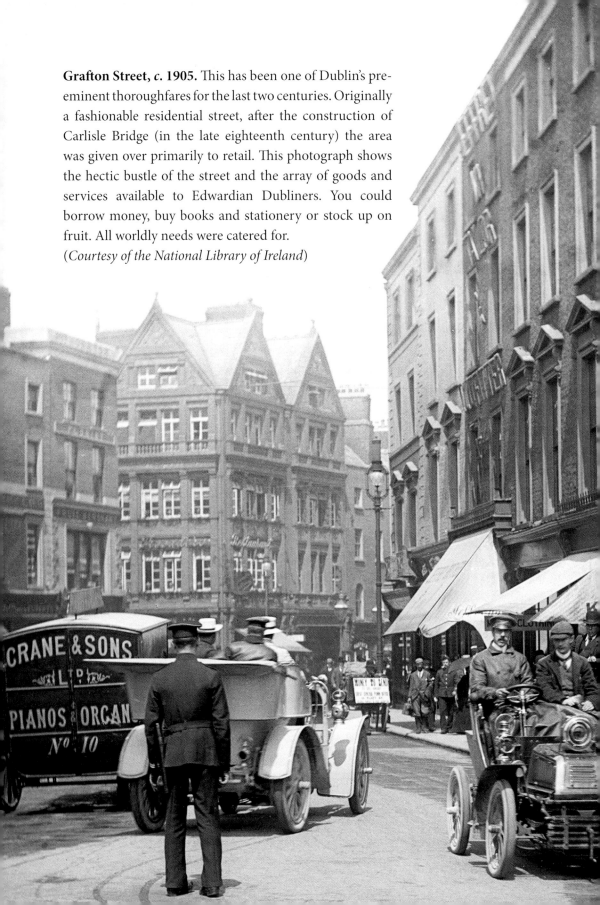

Grafton Street, *c*. 1905. This has been one of Dublin's pre-eminent thoroughfares for the last two centuries. Originally a fashionable residential street, after the construction of Carlisle Bridge (in the late eighteenth century) the area was given over primarily to retail. This photograph shows the hectic bustle of the street and the array of goods and services available to Edwardian Dubliners. You could borrow money, buy books and stationery or stock up on fruit. All worldly needs were catered for.
(*Courtesy of the National Library of Ireland*)

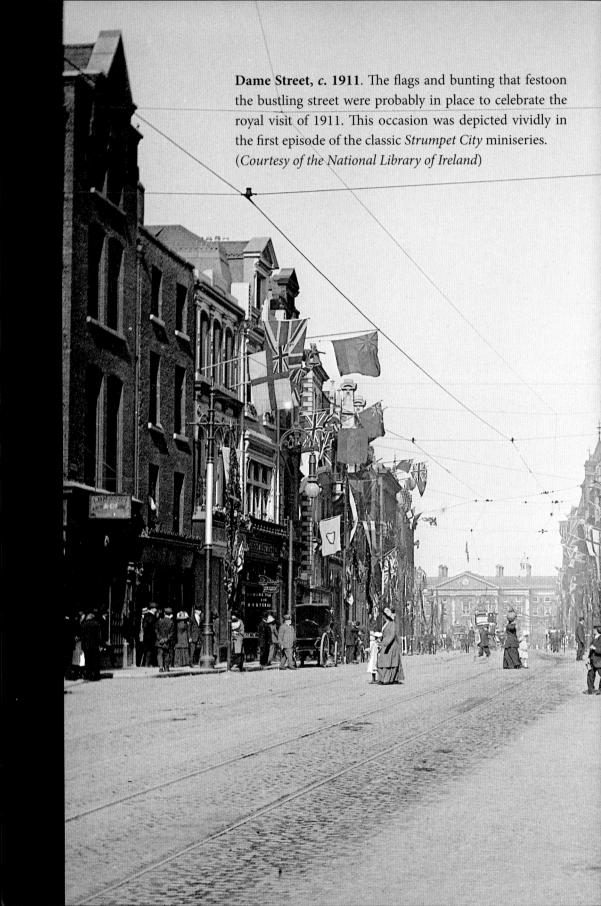

Dame Street, *c.* 1911. The flags and bunting that festoon the bustling street were probably in place to celebrate the royal visit of 1911. This occasion was depicted vividly in the first episode of the classic *Strumpet City* miniseries. (*Courtesy of the National Library of Ireland*)

O'Connell Bridge, *c.* 1920s. Much of Sackville Street was damaged during the Easter Rising of 1916 and the street hadn't been fully repaired before fighting during the Civil War brought even more destruction. This photograph, taken post-independence, shows a street returned to its former glory and vitality, but missing a few of its earlier iconic features.

(*Courtesy of the Ken Finlay Collection*)

COMMERCIAL DUBLIN

This chapter answers two important questions about Dublin around the turn of the twentieth century: what did you do to earn a few bob and what could you do with a few bob? It gives a glimpse into the working lives of contemporary Dubliners and also depicts some of the goods available in the city's stores at the time.

Grafton Street, Dublin.

THE NEW MART, SACKVILLE STREET.

THE SUBSCRIBERS beg respectfully to announce that the First Division of their new Premises
WILL BE OPENED FOR BUSINESS ON
SATURDAY, the 28th INST,

When they purpose exhibiting a large and varied Stock of the Newest and Choicest Goods in the following Departments, viz—
BRITISH AND FOREIGN SILKS, FRENCH, GERMAN, AND PAISLEY SHAWLS.

The Newest and Most Fashionable Designs in

MANTLES,	RIBBONS,	MUSLINS,	LINENS,	HABERDASHERY,
MILLINERY,	GLOVES,	FANCY DRESSES,	CALICOES,	TRIMMINGS,
FLOWERS,	HOSIERY,	PRINTS,	SHEETINGS,	PERFUMERY,
BONNETS,	LACES,	CASHMERES,	FLANNELS,	CABINET WARE,
PARASOLS,	BABY LINEN,	DE LAINES,	BLANKETS,	FANCY GOODS.

GENTLEMEN's FANCY HANDKERCHIEFS, TIES, SHIRTS, OUTFITS, &c, &c.

Dublin, May 21st, 1853.

McSWINEY, DELANY, AND CO.

The New Mart, Sackville Street. This advertisement announces the opening of the New Mart by McSwiney, Delaney, and Co., and shows the various and wide-ranging wares it offered at the time. The advertisement appeared in a publication promoting the Great Industrial Exhibition of 1853, which was a landmark trade expo and international event of its day, even attracting a royal visit. Some thirty years later the store was purchased by Michael J. Clery, who attached his name to it. The façade was all that survived the Easter Rising of 1916, although it was extended in the rebuilding and some new features were added.
(*Courtesy of Clerys Heritage Gallery*)

Giuseppe Cervi's Fried Fish and Chip Shop. Pride of place in this postcard of Great Brunswick Street (now Pearse Street) is Giuseppe Cervi's Fried Fish and Chip Shop at No. 22. Fish and chip shops are so ubiquitous in Dublin nowadays that it is hard to believe that they were only introduced in the 1880s. As far as I can ascertain, Giuseppe Cervi's was the first in Dublin.
(*Courtesy of the Ken Finlay Collection*)

Overleaf: **Taylor & Evans, Main Street, Malahide, *c.* 1901.** This prosperous-looking butcher's shop would make a modern-day food hygiene inspector faint. At the turn of the twentieth century it was standard for meat to be displayed outside butcher shops as shown. A young child peering out from the upstairs right-hand window suggests that, as was common during that era, one or other of the shop's proprietors lived in the dwelling upstairs.
(*Courtesy of Malahide Historical Society*)

Kingstown Harbour in the 1890s. The harbour at what is now Dún Laoghaire was enclosed in the 1820s. Due to the often treacherous conditions at the mouth of the Liffey, Kingstown Harbour was designed to safely accommodate ships bound for Dublin. In the years since, Dún Laoghaire (renamed in 1920) has served as a major passenger port for ships bound for Britain, as well as a fishing and leisure hub.
(*Courtesy of the Library of Congress, LC-DIG-ppmsc-009881*)

12106. - KINGSTOWN, CO. DUBLIN

Kingstown Harbour in the 1890s. This image, like several others in this collection, uses the Photochrom technique of colouring black-and-white images, invented in Switzerland in the 1880s and popular in the 1890s, before true colour photographic reproduction became commercially viable. Like the other Photochrom images in this book, this image was issued by the Detroit Printing Company.
(*Courtesy of the Library of Congress, LC-DIG-ppmsc-009880*)

12105. - KINGSTOWN HARBOUR.

Above: **Construction work near St Augustine Street, 1890.** This photograph was one of a series taken by James Talbot Power that documented the lives of working-class Dubliners who lived near the John's Lane whiskey distillery in the 1880s and 1890s. It shows the still basic methods used for construction at the time and suggests that women and children were employed at the very least in some ancillary role on the site.

(*Courtesy of the National Library of Ireland*)

Cabbie smoking a pipe, Westmoreland Street, *c*. 1903. There is a long-standing tradition in Dublin of the 'character'. They are eccentric, ostentatious or just interesting individuals who are fixtures on the city streets and add colour to the city's life. This gentleman looks like a character, who had probably seen and heard a lot of interesting things in his career as a cabbie. He is wearing his identification badge, either no. 1708 or 1798.
(*Courtesy of the National Library of Ireland*)

Opposite: **Smyth & Company's hosiery factory.** This stereo view image from 1903 shows the shop floor at the famous Smyth & Company's factory. Worn by British royalty, among others, 'Balbriggans' were a top international brand for much of the nineteenth and early twentieth centuries. The textiles industry around Balbriggan was a rare example of industrial development in the Dublin area in the nineteenth and early twentieth centuries. Stereo views were sold internationally and provided a three-dimensional image when viewed with a special apparatus.
(*Courtesy of the Fingal Local Studies Collection*)

Anglesea Market, c. 1909. The Moore Street area has been an iconic part of Dublin's commercial life for centuries. Anglesea Market, which was on Coles Lane, was established in 1826. Coles Lane was a street that ran parallel to Moore Street. It disappeared with the building of the Ilac Centre in 1981. (*Reproduced by permission of the Royal Society of Antiquaries of Ireland*)

Todd, Burns & Co. Ltd advertisement, 1905, from *The Leader* newspaper. The increasingly vociferous nationalism in Dublin and throughout Ireland in the late nineteenth and early twentieth centuries found expression in a number of ways, including the emphasis on Irish manufactured goods. This advertisement for the then newly opened Todd, Burns & Co. department store lists its various Irish-made goods. Todd, Burns & Co. was a significant retail concern in Dublin from the early nineteenth century until well into the twentieth century. In more recent times this premises has housed the first, flagship outlet of the internationally successful Penneys (Primark) chain of stores.

Lower Grafton Street. This coloured postcard from *c.* 1905 shows the handsome block of retail establishments along one side of the northern part of Grafton Street that lies between Suffolk Street and College Green. The side of the front entrance to Trinity College can be seen to the right, and in the distance the Dublin Bread Company's landmark building on Lower Sackville Street can also be discerned.
(*Courtesy of the Ken Finlay Collection*)

Sláinte cigarettes advertisement, 1905, from *The Leader* newspaper. Another advertisement attempting to cash in on nationalist fervour in Dublin at this time. It's ironic in retrospect that the manufacturers chose to call their product *Sláinte*, the Irish word for health. The Greenville factory was located near Harold's Cross, the company having relocated its manufacturing there after a catastrophic fire at their original Tullamore plant in 1886.

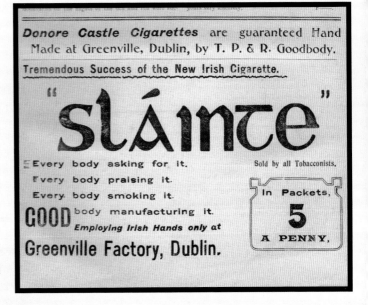

49

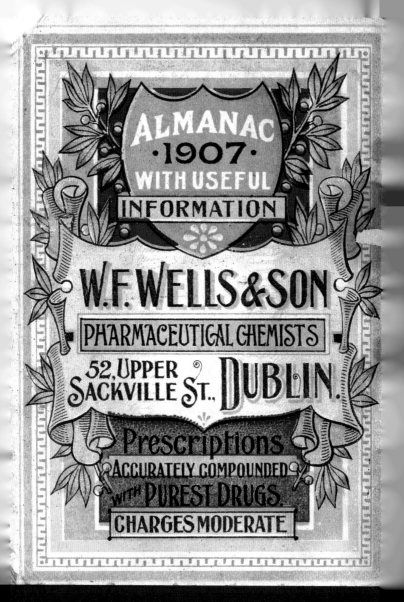

...lls advertisement. W. F. Wells & Son was established in Sackville ...by the 1880s the firm also had premises at 20 Upper Baggot Street. ...ucts such as Wells' Balsamic Cough Elixir, which promised a spe... ...s, colds, hoarseness and influenza!

Market Street Storehouse, *c.* 1906–10. No section on Dublin's commercial life could be complete without a mention of the beverage behemoth that is Guinness. This image shows the Market Street Storehouse at the south end of the St James's Gate Brewery complex shortly after it was built in 1904. This imposing building was in continuous use until the 1980s. Nowadays it houses the popular Guinness Storehouse attraction, which serves as a museum about Arthur Guinness and the history of the famous product, as well as outlining the industrial process involved in creating the black stuff. (*Courtesy of Diageo Ireland*)

Cask-filling department at the Guinness Brewery, *c.* 1910. This postcard shows men hard at work in the vast Guinness Brewery, filling casks with the famous black stuff. (*Courtesy of the Ken Finlay Collection*)

Above: **Draymen, St James's Gate Brewery, *c*. 1885–87.** This photograph shows Guinness employees in the stable yard at the brewery posing proudly with their drays and horses. Draymen, as ambassadors of the firm on the streets of Dublin, were expected to keep their horses, drays and selves well presented. Around this time Guinness kept about 150 horses to deliver their product to thirsty Dubliners. (*Courtesy of Diageo Ireland*)

Guinness advertisement, 1953. Although slightly later than the rest of the images in this book, it would be a crime to exclude one of the most iconic images ever created for a Dublin firm. This colourful advertisement for Guinness features the famous Guinness toucan. Devised in the 1930s at a London ad agency, the toucan remains a popular and instantly recognisable mascot of the world-famous Dublin beverage, and can be seen adorning many a Dublin pub.
(*Courtesy of Diageo Ireland*)

Opposite: **Steamers at the Custom House.** Barges brought barrels of Guinness from a special wharf on the Liffey near St James's Gate down to Custom House Quay for transfer to ships that carried the precious cargo to the thirsty masses of Britain and beyond. They were a regular sight on the river from the 1870s until they ceased to be used in June 1961.
(*Courtesy of the Ken Finlay Collection*)

Left: **No. 3 Elm Park, Ranelagh, *c.* 1910.** This card, presumably produced as a promotional tool, shows that this confectionary shop sold perennial favourites like Cadbury's and Fry's Chocolate, as well as a host of other treats. As was common at the time, the proprietor lived above the shop.

Below: **Henry Street, *c.* 1910.** The World's Fair Stores offered goods at the princely sum of 6½ pence, as well as a waxwork exhibition and 'Grand Variety Entertainment'. This prosperous block of shops, along the south side of Henry Street, was another casualty of the 1916 Rising. Backing onto the GPO, all the shops here were destroyed in the fighting. (*Both images courtesy of the Ken Finlay Collection*)

Selling newspapers at Kingstown. This postcard of Kingstown's Carlisle Pier is most notable for the inclusion of Davy Stephens, a newspaper salesman. He is the elderly gentleman holding a newspaper beside the lamp post at the bottom of the image. Davy sold newspapers to people getting on and off the mail boat at Kingstown for over fifty years. He counted British royalty among the thousands of friends and acquaintances he made down through the years.

(*Courtesy of the Ken Finlay Collection*)

Mespil Road. It took a while to identify exactly where this photograph was taken, as right behind where these men are congregating there now stands a handsome red-brick building, constructed in 1916. For forty years from 1949 the building housed perhaps Dublin's most important bookshop, Parson's. Patrick Kavanagh, Brendan Behan, Brian O'Nolan and other luminaries of the mid-century Dublin literary scene frequented the shop.

(*Courtesy of the Ken Finlay Collection*)

Silk and Millinery departments, pre-1916. This photograph gives a glimpse of the opulent Victorian interiors of Clerys in the years before the building's destruction during the 1916 Rising, as well as the fine goods it purveyed at the time.
(*Courtesy of Clerys Heritage Gallery*)

***Opposite*: Brown Thomas advertisement, 1922.** Brown Thomas has been a fixture on Grafton Street since Hugh Brown opened his store at No. 16 in 1848. The iconic Brown Thomas name was a result of a later partnership with James Thomas. This advertisement, which appeared in *Dublin Opinion* in December 1922, shows the array of Christmas gifts available for the better-off children of Dublin. Appearing at the height of the Civil War, ads such as this show that, insofar as was possible, Dubliners' lives went on as normal during this turbulent period. Brown Thomas continues to occupy a prominent place in Dublin commercial life.
(*Courtesy of the Ken Finlay Collection*)

BROWN THOMAS

CHRISTMAS BAZAAR NOW IN FULL SWING

Bring the Children to see "Puss in the Well." Santa Claus will be here to meet them

Brown Thomas & Co., Ltd., Grafton Street, Dublin

Findlater's, 67 South Great George's Street. This store appeared to stock everything required to have a most agreeable Christmas. Stockings hang in the window, while a sign for turkeys can be seen on the opposite side. Above the three men posing in the doorway, at least one of whom looks to be a staff member in his white apron, Christmas garlands hang. Originally from Scotland, Alexander Findlater came to Dublin in 1823. He started off in the whiskey business but subsequently expanded his company to include trade in a wide variety of goods. Findlater also owned shares in the St Lawrence Hotel in Howth and the Royal Hotel in Bray.
(*Courtesy of Dublin City Library and Archive*)

Opposite: **Kennedy's Bread advertisement, 1922.** Peter Kennedy was established as a 'fancy baker' as early as the mid-1850s in Great Britain Street (later Parnell Street). His bakery continued to operate right up until the early 1970s. Con Colbert, one of those executed in the aftermath of the Easter Rising, worked as a clerk for Kennedy's.
(*Courtesy of Dublin City Library and Archive*)

Finest Quality Made

KENNEDY'S

KING OF THE CASTLE

BREAD

Port of Dublin, 1930. Ireland was slow to develop economically after independence, but as can be seen in this postcard, Dublin was not devoid of industry. The port at the time was a major conduit for Irish livestock, food and drink to its export markets in Britain and further afield. The area also housed depots for many of the goods imported into Ireland such as coal and tobacco. However, at this point, Ireland's biggest export remained its people. In the top right of the photograph can be seen the train depot that in more recent times has become a popular live venue and is now known as the 3Arena.
(*Courtesy of the Ken Finlay Collection*)

Opposite: **Dublin Gas Company advertisement, 1939, *Irish Press*.** Formed in 1866, the Dublin Gas Company dominated the coal and gas market in Ireland for around 100 years. This imaginative and cosy advertisement appeared in newspapers just on the cusp of the Second World War. As a neutral nation, Ireland did not suffer to the extent any of the combatant nations did but there were widespread shortages, including of gas, as the war interrupted international trade. Anyone availing of the gas fire in their bedroom would have found themselves fearing the wrath of the Glimmer Man! (This was the colloquial term for inspectors who checked gas usage in homes during the Emergency.) The arrival of natural gas in Dublin in the latter part of the twentieth century bankrupted the company.

EVERY NIGHT HE'S ON THE HORNS OF A **DILEMMA**

The clock and his conscience say 'up to bed with you'! His book and pipe and cosy chair say 'wait a while before you face that chilly bedroom.' And so he sits deliberating, trying to muster up enough courage to leave the fireside. Someone should tell him that (provided he is a coin meter user) he could have a gas fire in his bedroom for 2/6 down.

GAS Fires MAKE BEDROOMS HEALTHY AND MORE INVITING !

DUBLIN GAS COMPANY

Zoological Gardens Phoenix Park Dubli[n]

DUBLIN AT PLAY

In a time when there were no TVs or computers, Dublin was well equipped to entertain its population. From outdoor spaces like St Stephen's Green, the Island Golf Club and Dublin's various beaches, to entertainments like the races, Dublin Zoo and GAA matches, with of course the ubiquitous Dublin pubs, there was plenty to do no matter what your tastes.

The Shelbourne Hotel and St Stephen's Green, *c.* 1890s. Dublin was, and still is, well supplied with parks where the population could spend their idle hours, but St Stephen's Green is probably the most famous of these. In this image the ladies and gentlemen whiling away an afternoon by the pond were enjoying a relatively new experience, as the park had only opened to the general public in 1880. The

Shelbourne, perhaps Dublin's most famous hotel, has been operating at this site on the Green since 1824 but was closed temporarily in the 1860s for extensive renovation. Due to mature trees along the perimeter, the Green no longer affords such a clear view of the hotel.

(*Courtesy of the Library of Congress, LC-DIG-ppmsc-09875*)

Blackrock Park, early 1900s. This park looks much the same today as it did in these postcards. The area now known as Blackrock Park was originally called the People's Park. It was reclaimed from slob land previously owned by the Earl of Pembroke. The earl gave the land to the Blackrock Town Commissioners in the 1870s with the understanding it would be converted to public use. The original Victorian features seen in these postcards, including the bandstand below, remain in place, but sadly many have fallen into a state of neglect in recent times.
(*Courtesy of the Ken Finlay Collection*)

Sorrento Park, early 1900s. This park, opened formally in 1894, formed part of the grounds of Sorrento House, the pre-eminent house on the nearby Sorrento Terrace. It was given as a gift by Lady MacDonnell to the town and put under the Dalkey Township Commissioners' care. In the latter part of the nineteenth century there was a trend for privately owned city and town gardens to be opened up for the enjoyment of all.

(*Courtesy of the Ken Finlay Collection*)

The Botanic Gardens, Glasnevin, *c*. 1890s. From their foundation in 1795, the Botanic Gardens have enjoyed immense popularity with leisure-seeking Dubliners, as well as being a centre for agricultural and botanical scientific inquiry. The signature curvilinear glasshouses were the work of the great Dublin ironmaster Richard Turner in the 1840s. Turner was also responsible for the Palm House in Belfast's Botanic Gardens.
(*Courtesy of the National Library of Ireland (photograph) and the Ken Finlay Collection (postcard)*)

Howth. The seaside was also a popular day out, and Dublin's coastline provided numerous choices. To the north of the city is Howth, where these ladies are taking in the sights and sounds of the East Pier. A mast can be seen atop the Martello Tower in the background. In 1903 the tower was used as the site for Lee de Forest's successful wireless radio experiments between Howth and Holyhead. De Forest was an American inventor and radio pioneer. The Martello Tower nowadays houses a popular radio museum. The more adventurous visitor could take a dip in the sea at Balscadden Bay (*below*), which remains a popular spot for swimming today.
(*Courtesy of the Ken Finlay Collection (top); Fingal Local Studies Collection (bottom)*)

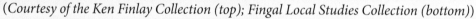

Bathing Strand, Howth

The Strand, Killiney, *c*. 1920s. This postcard shows a lovely summer's day some-time in the 1920s. The stony crescent beach's appeal is self-evident and the various amusements, distractions and refreshments must have made for a very pleasant day out indeed. Despite the popularity of foreign beach holidays in recent times, Killiney and other Dublin beaches still attract droves of visitors when the weather is suitable. (*Courtesy of the Ken Finlay Collection*)

Killiney Beach, *c*. 1920s. These ladies look to have been enjoying a lovely day at the beach. Their bathing attire is suitably fashionable for the period. (*Courtesy of Orla Fitzpatrick/jacolette.com*)

Bray Promenade, *c.* 1890s: To the south of Dublin city lies Bray, most of which is situated in Co. Wicklow. A mile-long walk along the seafront, Bray Promenade was built by engineer William Dargan as part of his plan to turn Bray into a popular seaside resort. His endeavours earned Bray the title The Brighton of Ireland. (*Courtesy of the Library of Congress, LC-DIG-ppmsc-09938*)

Above: **Kingstown Harbour and Promenade.** On the way back to the city from Bray was Kingstown Harbour and Promenade. Renamed Dún Laoghaire in 1920, this postcard appears to postdate that time. The attire of the women at the centre of the postcard suggests the image may have been captured in or around 1930. Whenever precisely it was, it must have been a lovely day, as the promenade is packed with people. On the left, in the background, the mail boat is docked.
(*Courtesy of the Ken Finlay Collection*)

***Above*: Kingstown Regatta.** The annual Kingstown Regatta attracted large crowds, as this image from the late 1890s shows. The spectators are wearing a fine cross-section of the hats then in vogue among Dublin's well-to-do. The regatta has a curious place in the history of sports and telecommunications. In 1898 Guglielmo Marconi radioed in results from a steam tug out on the bay, which were then telephoned in from the shore to the *Dublin Express* offices in Dublin city centre. It is claimed that this was the first live sports broadcast in history.

(*Originally published in John F. Finnerty,* Ireland in Pictures *(J. S. Hyland & Co., 1898)*)

***Opposite*: Kingstown Pavilion.** Another attraction available to the visitor in this bustling harbour was the Kingstown Pavilion. This pretty wooden structure, constructed in 1903, housed tea rooms, a sunroom and a concert hall which hosted performances by both local luminaries and international acts. One contemporary guidebook described it as 'one of the most picturesque pavilions in the United Kingdom'. Sadly, it burned down in 1915.

(*Courtesy of the Ken Finlay Collection*)

Dublin Zoological Gardens, *c.* 1900. Dublin Zoo, in the heart of Phoenix Park, has been a much-loved institution since its foundation in 1831. It has been claimed that during the Easter Rising, when there were food shortages at the zoo, other animals were killed and fed to the lions and tigers. For reasons lost to history, this camel's handler appears none too happy. Perhaps he was on clean-up duty that day. (*Courtesy of the National Library of Ireland*)

Below: A camel also appears in this Edwardian-era postcard from *c.* 1905. The zoo's ever-changing array of weird and wonderful creatures, has captured the hearts of millions of visitors down the years. The zoo was also the inspiration for the earthy ballad 'The Zoological Gardens', most famously sung by the Dubliners in the 1960s. (*Courtesy of the Ken Finlay Collection*)

Zoological Gardens Phoenix Park Dublin

IN THE ZOO. DUBLIN.

THE SCALP, C? DUBLIN.

E55.
J.J.M.

The Scalp. For those Dubliners who wished to venture slightly farther afield, The Scalp, a chasm on Barnaslingan, a hill in South Dublin that borders County Wicklow, provided a picturesque day out. The hills and mountains of South Dublin and neighbouring Wicklow have been popular recreation spots for the last 200 years. (*Courtesy of the Ken Finlay Collection*)

Above and overleaf: **The Irish International Exhibition, Herbert Park, Ballsbridge.** These glass lantern slides depict scenes from the International Exhibition of 1907. As well as permanent attractions, there were also temporary events to pique people's interest. This 'great white city', as Bram Stoker dubbed the array of temporary exhibition spaces, gave several million visitors a glimpse at the state of the industrial arts as well as wonders from throughout the world. William Martin Murphy, the businessman and media mogul, was the main driving force behind the exhibition. Its only surviving physical remnants are the bandstand and pond in Herbert Park. *(Courtesy of the Representative Church Body Library/RCB Library Killaloe lantern*

The Horse Show, Ballsbridge, 1890s. Horses have always been a popular part of Irish life, and there were various leisure events where Dubliners could enjoy these animals. The Dublin Horse Show is an immensely popular equestrian showjumping event that began in 1864. Originally held on the lawns of Leinster House, it has been held annually in Ballsbridge since 1881. This image shows off what was in fashion for well-heeled *fin de siècle* Dubliners and visitors from farther afield. Governments and armies throughout the world often sought Irish thoroughbreds because of their quality.
(*Originally published in John F. Finnerty,* Ireland in Pictures *(J. S. Hyland & Co., 1898)*)

Fingal Harriers. For those who owned their own horses, there was of course always the hunt to look forward to. Although hunting is not as popular today as it was in the past, groups such as the Fingal Harriers, formed in 1881, continue their hunt traditions across Dublin's rural hinterland. These two people, pictured here in front of Swords Castle, were part of a hunt some time around 1940.
(*Courtesy of Swords Museum*)

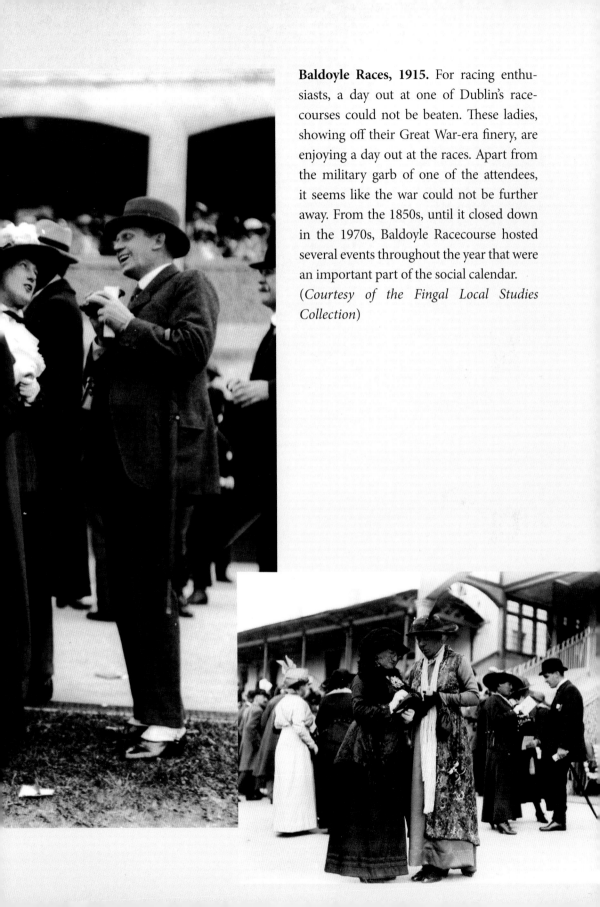

Baldoyle Races, 1915. For racing enthusiasts, a day out at one of Dublin's racecourses could not be beaten. These ladies, showing off their Great War-era finery, are enjoying a day out at the races. Apart from the military garb of one of the attendees, it seems like the war could not be further away. From the 1850s, until it closed down in the 1970s, Baldoyle Racecourse hosted several events throughout the year that were an important part of the social calendar. (*Courtesy of the Fingal Local Studies Collection*)

Kenilworth Bowling Club, Grosvenor Square, c. 1910. For those looking for a more energetic pastime, there was, of course, a wide array of sports to choose from. A group of gentlemen of the lawn-bowling persuasion got together in 1892 and formed a bowling club at Kenilworth Square. That square proving unsuitable for their needs, the club moved to Grosvenor Square in 1909, where it is still based to this day. Lawn bowls maintains a small but loyal following across Dublin.
(*Courtesy of the Ken Finlay Collection*)

The Island Golf Club, early 1900s. Golf exploded in popularity in Ireland in the 1890s. By the end of the century there were approximately 100 courses throughout the country. The Island Golf Club, one of the oldest in Ireland, was established in 1890 and sits on a sandy peninsula in Donabate, opposite Malahide, on Malahide Estuary. Originally the golf links were accessed by boat from Malahide, but the ferry service was discontinued in the 1970s. Membership was initially limited to Protestants of a certain social background. These images show William Francis Moore, one of its founders, as well as some early lady golfers.
(*Courtesy of the Fingal Local Studies Collection*)

Michael Collins and Harry Boland playing hurling, Croke Park, 11 September 1921. After the foundation of the Gaelic Athletic Association in 1884, the sports of Gaelic football and hurling went from strength to strength. In this image, two icons of the Irish republican movement, Michael Collins and Harry Boland, are clearly having fun practising their hurling skills at the Leinster Hurling Final, although they are both rather overdressed for it! This playful scene is lent great poignancy by the knowledge that both men would die violent deaths, on opposing sides of the Civil War, in less than a year.

(*Courtesy of the National Library of Ireland*)

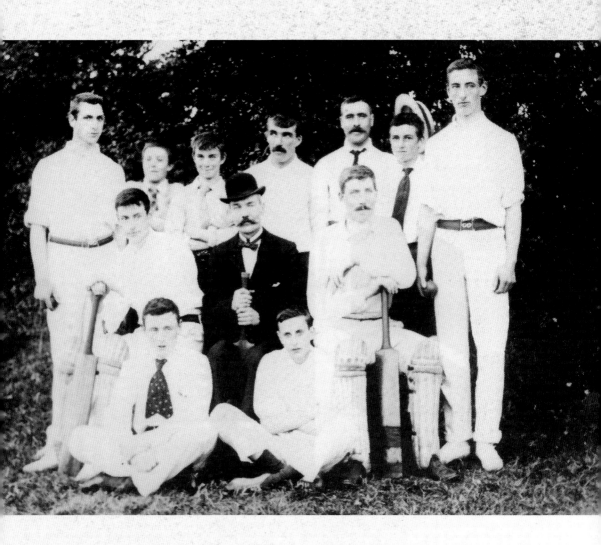

Malahide Cricket Team, 1901. Cricket has been a popular sport in Malahide and elsewhere in Dublin for over 150 years. Malahide Cricket Club was founded in 1861 and is still going strong today. This photograph shows the team from 1901 (*starting top left*): T. Kettle, A. Lawler, F. Lawler, D. O'Brien, C. O'Connor, E. Crowley, C. Adams; A. Adams (vice-captain), J. Stubbings (umpire), D. Campion (captain); H. Holton and H. Robinson. Tom Kettle was later Irish Parliamentary Party MP for East Tyrone. He fought with the Royal Dublin Fusiliers in the First World War and died at Picardy in 1916. A statue in his memory stands in St Stephen's Green. (*Courtesy of Malahide Cricket Club*)

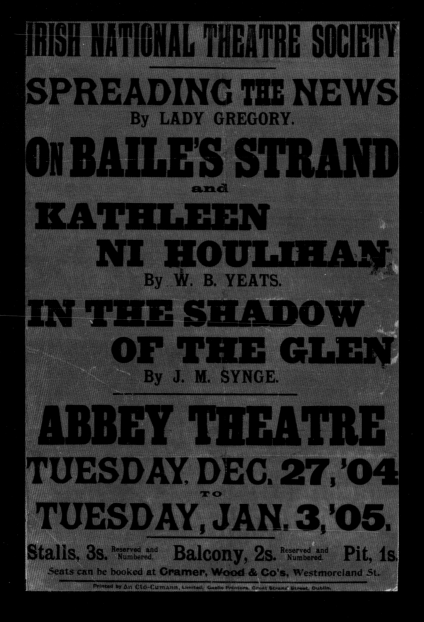

Abbey Theatre poster, December 1904. Dublin's theatres have long played an important role in entertaining its citizens. Leading lights of contemporary Irish theatre, including W. B. Yeats, Lady Gregory and J. M. Synge, were involved in the Abbey Theatre's foundation in 1904, although it would never have seen the light of day without the financial backing of Annie Horniman, an English theatre manager and administrator. Initially the theatre was a success, drawing huge crowds of Dubliners. However, an early upset occurred in January 1907, when the opening of Synge's *Playboy of the Western World* was met with riots. Despite this and other tribulations down the years, the Abbey has long since taken its place as Ireland's national theatre and maintains a high reputation to the present day.
(*Courtesy of the National Library of Ireland*)

Theatre Royal, Hawkins Street. There have been a number of Theatre Royals in Dublin down through the years. The first one opened in 1662 in Smock Alley. The second was located on Hawkins Street but burned down in 1880. The one pictured is the third of that name, constructed in 1897. It began primarily as an opera house, reflecting the immense popularity of opera in the city at that time, but later diversified into music hall and cinema presentations. A teenage, and as yet unknown, Charles Chaplin performed here in 1906 as part of a music hall troupe. The theatre closed in March 1934. Another Theatre Royal was built on this spot in 1935 in the Art Deco style, but it was demolished in 1962 and replaced by a grim block of civil service offices.

(Courtesy of the National Library of Ireland)

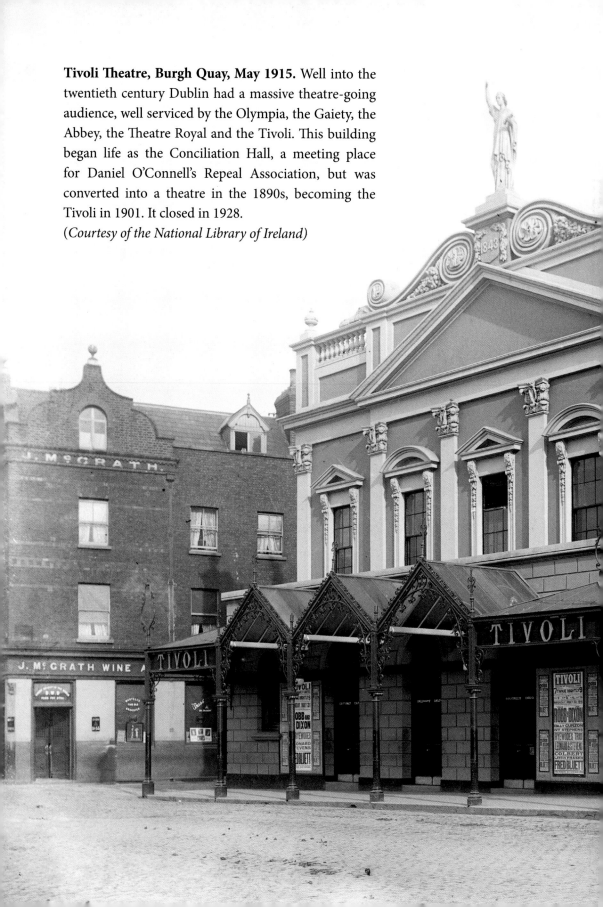

Tivoli Theatre, Burgh Quay, May 1915. Well into the twentieth century Dublin had a massive theatre-going audience, well serviced by the Olympia, the Gaiety, the Abbey, the Theatre Royal and the Tivoli. This building began life as the Conciliation Hall, a meeting place for Daniel O'Connell's Repeal Association, but was converted into a theatre in the 1890s, becoming the Tivoli in 1901. It closed in 1928.
(*Courtesy of the National Library of Ireland*)

GAIETY THEATRE
DUBLIN

BLUE BEARD

PANTOMIME
BOOK OF WORDS

PRICE SIXPENCE.

Cahill Designers & Printers Dublin.

Gaiety performances. The Gaiety Theatre, which opened in 1871, is still well known for its Christmas pantomimes, and in 1886 it was Bluebeard that no doubt delighted the children of Dublin. The programme below, from 1939, would probably have been one more for the adults. The Ballet Rambert was the first repertory ballet in Britain and, as the Rambert Dance Company, continues to thrive. (*Courtesy of Dublin City Library and Archive*)

GAIETY THEATRE, DUBLIN

Telephone : DUBLIN 22205

FOR TWO WEEKS ONLY

Opening Monday, July 24th

Evenings at 8   *Matinées Saturdays, 2.30*

First Visit of the

BALLET RAMBERT

in a Repertoire of Sixteen Ballets

with

NINA GOLOVINA	WALTER GORE
ELISABETH SCHOOLING	FRANK STAFF
SALLY GILMOUR	TRAVIS KEMP
SUSETTE MORFIELD	CHARLES BOYD

AND CORPS DE BALLET

Musicians :
EDWIN BENBOW & ANGUS MORRISON

Direction : MARIE RAMBERT

GAIETY THEATRE

DUBLIN

'PANTOMIME'

The Rotunda Cinema, 1913. Another popular form of indoor entertainment for Dubliners were the 'new living pictures' shown in cinemas such as the Rotunda at the top of Sackville Street. Originally built as an assembly hall for the Rotunda Hospital, the building was used intermittently for movie screenings between 1897 and 1908. In 1910 it became a full-time cinema and continued in this role (later renamed the Ambassador) until 1999. Also in the photograph is the Augustus Saint-Gaudens' sculpted Parnell monument, unveiled only two years previously.
(*Courtesy of the National Library of Ireland*)

DINE AT THE —

Dolphin Hotel

. AND .

Restaurant.

Essex St. (Parliament Street), **Dublin.**

Dolphin Hotel advertisement, *The Lepracaun* **magazine, 1909.** The Dolphin Hotel was not the best hotel in Dublin at the time, with its more famous rivals such as the Shelbourne vying for that accolade. Its restaurant, however, was regarded as one of the best in the city and it enjoyed a great reputation as a watering hole. Some years later, in 1943, *Life* magazine named the Dolphin as the 'best bar in Dublin, and thus probably in the world'. However, time stands still for no business, and unfortunately the Dolphin went out of business some years ago. You can still, at least, admire its ornate Victorian façade on Essex Street East today, with the name still inscribed above the door. Like most of the advertisements that featured in the pages of *The Lepracaun*, this was illustrated by the talented Thomas Fitzpatrick.

THE ROCKY ROAD TO DUBLIN.

Sunday Morning—The Bona-fides returning from Finglas.

Bona Fide cartoon, *The Lepracaun* magazine, 1905. Another of Thomas Fitzpatrick's canon comically depicts those involved in what seems to be thought of internationally as not just Dublin's but Ireland's favourite pastime – drinking. At the time it was only permissible to drink after hours in Dublin if you were five or more miles from your residence, that is, a traveller. This exception was meant only for bona fide travellers, but resourceful drinkers like those depicted would head out of town to the likes of Phibsboro, Finglas, Kingstown or Santry and purport to be travellers in order to keep drinking! Such shenanigans only ended with the abolition of the bona fide exception in the Intoxicating Liquor Act of 1960.

The Blackhorse Tavern, early twentieth century. This postcard shows one example of Dublin's myriad watering holes. Variously known as the Blackhorse Tavern, the Hole in the Wall, and Nancy Hand's, the pub was (and indeed still is) located adjacent to Phoenix Park on Blackhorse Avenue. It appears that Nancy Hand was a famous proprietor of the establishment sometime in the nineteenth century. Her name is nowadays attached to another public house on Parkgate Street, on the other side of Phoenix Park.

The Original Hole in the Wall, Nancy Hands, Phoenix Park Dublin

The 'Hole in the Wall' appears to refer to the small gate that allows quick access between the park and the pub, although various stories have sprung up through the years about the provenance of the name. One such story suggested that at one time there was a hole in the park wall here, through which officials could anonymously receive bribes.

(*Courtesy of the Ken Finlay Collection*)

The Red Lion, South Great George's Street, 1909. This eye-catching advertisement, published in *The Lepracaun* magazine, trumpets the virtues of The Red Lion, an establishment on the ever-popular South Great George's Street, which has long since vanished. From the advertisement it is clear that this pub was a sister establishment to the Blue Lion, a favourite haunt of Sean O'Casey's, which is also, alas, no more.
(*Author's collection*)

MORAN'S TEMPERANCE HOTEL,

71 & 72, Lower Gardiner Street, & 20a & 20b, Talbot Street,
DUBLIN.

SITUATION most central being within two minutes walk of Great Northern Railway, Custom House, General Post office, and close to cross-Channel steamers, Trinity College, banks, public Offices, etc. Night Porter. *New Sanitary Drainage System, carried out under directions of*

W. KAYE PARRY,
M.A., C.E., etc.

Telegrams :
Moran's Hotel, Dublin.

Large, airy, and well-appointed Bed Billiard and Smoking Rooms
BEDS, **1/6** to **2/-** BREAKFASTS, from **1/-** to **1/6.**
DINNERS from **1/6** to **2/6** LIGHTED BY ELECTRICITY.
HOT AND COLD BATHS NO CHARGE FOR ATTENDANCE.
Telephone 914. J. MORAN, Proprietor.

Moran's Temperance Hotel, c. 1901. Of course, not everyone approved of the drinking culture at the time, and some hotels, like Moran's, refused to sell drink on the premises. It is interesting to see what the hotel emphasises in its advertisement – baths, electric light and elevators, all of which are a given to the modern consumer, are presented as selling points. And wouldn't we all love a telephone number that was only three digits!
(*Author's collection*)

Thomas Talbot Power, Mount Merrion, 1902. With the growing interest in motor cars, Dubliners could use their leisure time to venture further afield. On Sunday 17 August 1902, Thomas Talbot Power left Dublin on a tour to the south of the country. His party of five covered 902 miles in his 10 hp Wolseley, taking in the delights of Cork and Kerry on the trip. However, they did have some trouble finding petrol for the car, and Power reported that the condition of some of the roads in Kerry were 'not fit for any motor car'.
(*Courtesy of the RIAC Archive*)

IAC motor tour, Shelbourne Hotel, 1901. In 1901 a motoring tour of Ireland was organised by the newly formed Irish Automobile Club. Sixteen cars took part in the tour, which took in Waterford, Cork, Kerry, Clare and Connemara and lasted for fifteen days. The tour started outside the Shelbourne Hotel on 8 August and some of the participants can be seen here.
(*Courtesy of the RIAC Archive*)

Dublin place name cigarette cards. Entertainment in the home was more limited in the early twentieth century, but collecting was one activity that could while away some time. These cards, purportedly painted by Jack B. Yeats, were given away with packets of John Player and Sons cigarettes. They are part of two series of Irish place name cards, issued in 1927 and 1929. Cigarette cards were a popular promotional collectable from the 1870s until the 1940s. Many were issued with Irish interest subject matters such as GAA teams and scenic spots around the country.

(*Courtesy of the Fingal Local Studies Collection*)

PLAYER'S CIGARETTES

DUBLIN.   DUIBH-LINN.
DUBH'S POOL.

PLAYER'S CIGARETTES

SKERRIES.   SCEIRE.
SHARP SEA ROCKS.

PLAYER'S CIGARETTES

RUSH.   ROS-EÓ.
THE PENINSULA OF THE YEW-TREES.

PLAYER'S CIGARETTES

CHAPEL-IZOD.
THE CHAPEL OF ISOUD.

PLAYER'S CIGARETTES

KILLINEY.   CILL INGENA LENIN.
THE CHURCH OF THE DAUGHTERS OF LENIN.

PLAYER'S CIGARETTES

BOOTERSTOWN. BAILE-AN-BHOTHAIR.
THE TOWN OF THE ROAD.

PLAYER'S CIGARETTES

CLONTARF.   CLUAIN-TAIRBH.
BULL'S MEADOW.

Postcards. Postcards took off in popularity in the early 1900s and also became highly collectable. Often used as holiday souvenirs to send home, they were also popular for dropping friends and family a quick note in the days when phone calls were still largely the preserve of the very well off. The Milton Postcard Company issued many sets of postcards like this one for Dublin.
(*Courtesy of the Ken Finlay Collection*)

Sackville Street postcard. This kitsch representation of Sackville Street fits in with a Blarneyfied notion of Ireland that owes its genesis to the sentimental representations of Ireland popular with Irish migrant communities throughout the world in the second half of the nineteenth century. To a degree this vision is still sold to foreign tourists in the present day.
(*Courtesy of the Ken Finlay Collection*)

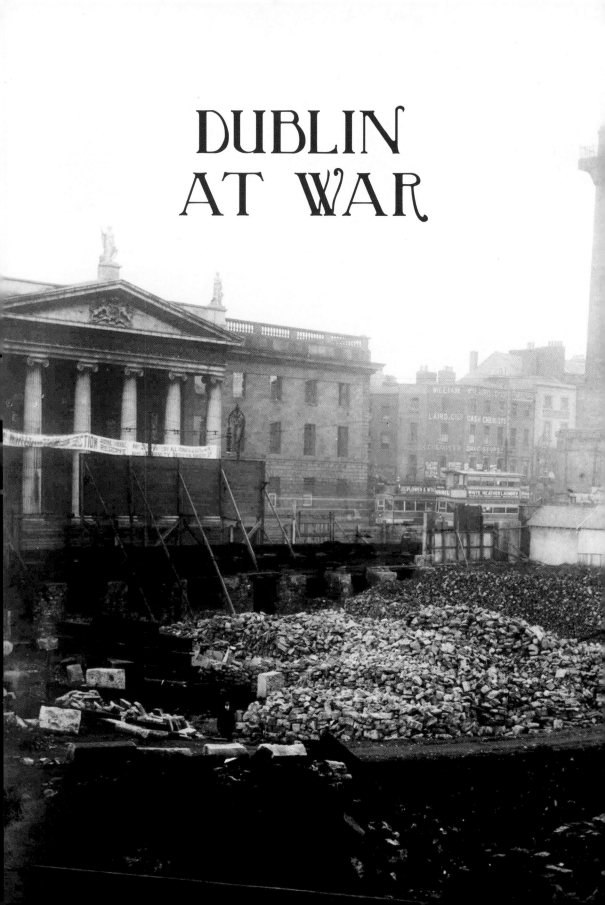

DUBLIN
AT WAR

The early twentieth century saw the city suffer two major catastrophes which caused widespread devastation to its iconic city centre – the 1916 Easter Rising and the Irish Civil War. Moreover, thousands of Dubliners fought and died in the First World War, and, as one of the UK's major cities, Dublin played its part in that war. This chapter also includes images of the British Army regiments which were based in the capital. As Dublin was the centre of the British administrative system in Ireland, it is not surprising that they, too, have left their mark on its landscape.

Scots Guards, Lord Edward Street, *c.* 1897. In this photograph a company of Scots Guards parades up Lord Edward Street. The 2nd Division of the Scots Guards were deployed to Ireland in 1895 and departed in 1897, replaced by the 1st Division. The company may well have been parading to mark Queen Victoria's diamond jubilee on 20 June 1897.

(*Originally published in John F. Finnerty,* Ireland in Pictures (*J. S. Hyland & Co., 1898*))

Veterans, Kilmainham, *c.* 1910. The Royal Hospital at Kilmainham, completed in 1684, was typically home to some 300 elderly and disabled veterans. It ceased operating as an old soldiers' home in 1927. Some of the veterans would have seen action in far-flung places like the Crimea, Afghanistan, New Zealand or India. The top image shows a veteran march, while the image below provides a glimpse of the richly decorated reading room at the hospital. At one time the Royal Hospital was intended to become the home of Dáil Éireann.
(*Courtesy of the Ken Finlay Collection*)

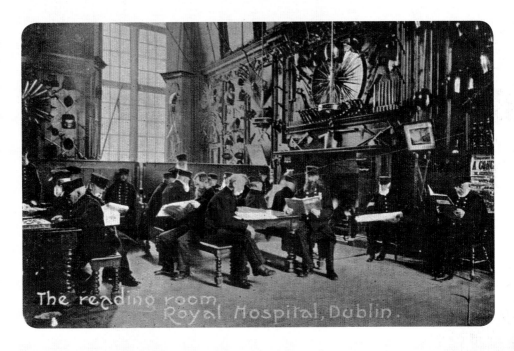

College Green, *c.* 1890. This scene shows the façade of Trinity College and a bustling College Green, with trams, horses and a group of Royal Dublin Fusiliers all vying for space. King William of Orange also puts in a cameo, in statue form. The Royal Dublin Fusiliers were formed in 1881 and the regiment was involved in many battles, including the Easter Rising, when three of its battalions were sent to attack the Irish nationalists. With the establishment of the Irish Free State the regiment was disbanded. (*Courtesy of the Library of Congress, LC-DIG-ppmsc-009879*)

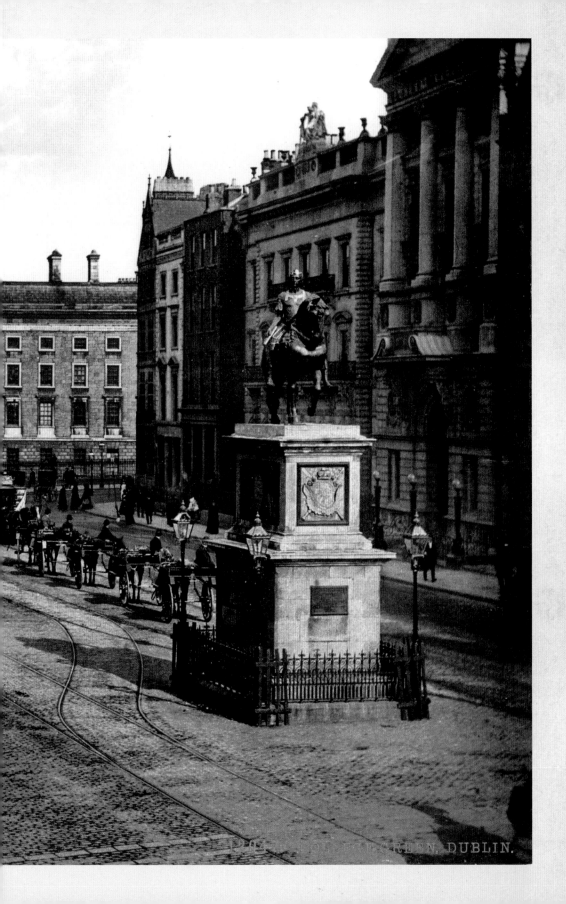

Below: **Marlborough Barracks, Cabra, early twentieth century.** Construction began on this building in 1888 and took four years to complete. It originally housed almost 900 horses. As home to the Equitation School, McKee Barracks remains a home to horses to this day. After independence, the barracks was renamed in honour of Richard McKee, a native of Finglas who fought in the War of Independence. McKee was killed alongside Peadar Clancy and Conor Clune in Dublin Castle on 21 November 1920, seemingly in retribution for the IRA's assassination of members of the Cairo Gang earlier that day. (*Courtesy of the Ken Finlay Collection*)

Changing of the Guard at Dublin Castle, *c*. 1905. This image captured the changing of the guard ceremony at Dublin Castle, then and for many years previously the nerve centre of British administration in Ireland. There is some uncertainty as to the uniforms worn, but it seems a group of Royal Irish Fusiliers are on the left and the men on the right are members of the Royal Irish Rifles.

(*Courtesy of the National Library of Ireland*)

Recruitment posters, 1915. Posters such as these, both printed and published by Dublin firms, were used to exhort Irishmen to sign up for the British Army during the Great War. While many Irishmen happily served in the British armed forces at the time, the debate over whether to join up exposed the division within Irish nationalism. The Irish Volunteers, formed in 1913, split into the John Redmond-led National Volunteers, who lent support to Britain's war effort, and the Irish Volunteers, who worked to achieve Irish independence.

(*Courtesy of the Library of Congress, LC-USZC4-11356 and LC-USZC4-10986*)

KILDARE HOUSE

SERVICE JACKET, in Regulation Whipcord or Serge, £2 15 0
Heavy Weight, £3 3 0

Soldiers' uniforms. Posters were not the only wartime items produced in Dublin. The men who were going off to fight needed uniforms, and Calvert and Company of

GREAT COAT, Cavalry or Infantry, £3 15 0
Best Quality, £4 4 0

Kildare House, 13 Westmoreland Street, was one of the firms which supplied them.
(*Courtesy of Dublin City Library and Archive*)

Thomas Ashe. Ashe was a leading light in the Irish Volunteers and led the Fingal (North Dublin) battalion. During the Easter Rising, which started on 24 April 1916 and was over by the following Sunday, the battalion's actions were some of the most significant outside Dublin city centre. In September 1917 Ashe, who had been incarcerated for sedition, went on hunger strike demanding prisoner-of-war status. He died as the result of a botched attempt to force-feed him. This memorial card comes from *c*. 1920. (*Courtesy of the Fingal Local Studies Collection*)

Fingal Volunteers, 1916. These men, under the leadership of Thomas Ashe, were involved in a raid on the Royal Irish Constabulary (RIC) barracks at Swords, as well as the more significant Battle of Ashbourne that took place on Friday 28 April 1916. (*Courtesy of Swords Museum*)

120

Henry Street, 1916 After the rebels surrendered, much of Dublin city centre lay in

Clerys. The photograph on the left gives some indication of the extent of the damage that the Clerys building sustained during Easter Week 1916. When the fighting ceased, all that remained of the historic building was the façade. It would be four years before the building was ready to be reopened. While the building was being reconstructed, the Clerys business operated out of a premises around the corner on Lower Abbey Street.

The advertisement above for the reopening of Clerys shows the building readers may be familiar with, although it appears to lack an essential feature, its famous clock. 'Under the clock at Clerys' has been a rendezvous point for lovers for generations. In the intervening ninety-odd years Clerys has gone through other tribulations, including being badly flooded in 2013, which forced its closure for four months. The business went into liquidation in June 2015 and, at the time of going to press, its future was far from certain.

(*Courtesy of Clerys Heritage Gallery*)

Lower Sackville Street, May 1916. A crowd surveys the damage. Much of the block from Eden Quay to Abbey Street was destroyed. The most prominent building, with its façade somewhat intact, is the Dublin Bread Company; unlike Clerys, it was not rebuilt. (*Courtesy of the National Library of Ireland*)

Auxiliary, Gloucester Street, February 1921. From 1919–21 the War of Independence raged across Ireland. The British government recruited two new forces, the Black and Tans and the Auxiliary Division, to help in the fight against the IRA. This fellow, smoking and posing with a Lewis machine gun, seems to be a member of the Auxiliary Division, popularly known as the Auxies. The Auxies largely consisted of ex-British officers, who were recruited into a paramilitary force to bolster the RIC. The Auxies and the Black and Tans became infamous for the atrocities they committed and the two forces are often confused in the popular memory.
(*Courtesy of the National Library of Ireland*)

North Western Hotel, North Wall Quay, *c.* **1907.** This handsome hotel was constructed for the London and North Western Railway Company in the 1880s to accommodate travellers from Holyhead on the company's steam packet service. During the War of Independence Auxiliaries were billeted there, and in April 1921 it was the scene of an unsuccessful attack by the IRA. The hotel

was later known as the British Rail Hotel. Following this it was taken over and used as offices by CIÉ. Although still intact, as of 2015 the building lies empty. (*Courtesy of the Ken Finlay Collection*)

Dublin Castle, *c.* **1920–21.** Barbed-wire defences and a sentry post outside the castle. As the security situation worsened during the war and British operatives were targeted for assassination by the IRA, military officers, civil servants and intelligence staff took up residence in the castle.
(*Courtesy of Mercier Archive*)

Civil War. Dublin once again suffered major destruction during the Civil War. The start of that conflict was heralded by an attack on Dublin's Four Courts (right, after its bombardment with heavy artillery), where the anti-Treaty IRA had set up their headquarters, on 28 June 1922. Civilians trying to go about their everyday lives suffered disruption as the new Free State Army attempted to root out anti-Treaty IRA men. In the image above, Free State soldiers are searching vehicles, although all involved seem rather relaxed as the driver grins for the camera.
(*Courtesy of Mercier Archive*)

129

St John Ambulance Men, *c.* 1922–23. It was not only combatants who suffered during the fierce fighting in Dublin during the Civil War. This photograph shows St John Ambulance men attempting to help an injured civilian. As well as coming to the aid of civilians, the St John Ambulance Brigade provided medical care to those fighting on both sides in the Civil War.

(*Courtesy of Mercier Archive*)

Gresham Hotel, Sackville Street, 1922. The fighting in Dublin came to an end on Wednesday 5 July 1922. The Gresham Hotel was one of the buildings on Sackville Street being used by the anti-Treaty IRA as a base of operations. By late Wednesday it was on fire and this photograph shows the level of destruction caused to the well-known hotel. It would be a number of years before Dublin was fully rebuilt. (*Courtesy of Mercier Archive*)

The Collins and Griffith Cenotaph, 1922. This temporary cenotaph was erected on Leinster Lawn, at the rear of Leinster House, as a memorial to the recently gunned down Michael Collins and to Arthur Griffith, who had died of heart failure only ten days before Collins was killed in August 1922. Two of the key instigators of Ireland's independence were gone. The tenor John McCormack, who is laying the wreath, was at the time perhaps the most famous Irish person beyond the political realm. McCormack enjoyed an enduring popularity during the first decades of the twentieth century and played concerts to rapt audiences worldwide.
(*Courtesy of the Library of Congress, LC-B2-6060-4*)

Armistice Day commemoration, College Green, 11 November 1924. This huge crowd, estimated at 50,000, gathered to commemorate Ireland's fallen in the Great War. A Celtic Cross was erected (*centre*), which stayed in place for a time until it was transported to Guillemont, France, where it still stands as a memorial to the dead of the 16th Irish Division. The crowd in this photograph shows that narratives suggesting Ireland's contribution to the Great War was forgotten post-independence do not tell the whole story.

(*Courtesy of the National Library of Ireland*)

DUBLIN AT WORSHIP

Dublin's churches are some of its most recognisable buildings and they are littered throughout the city and its suburbs, although some have been lost to posterity through destruction. More than any other type of building they reflect the changing styles of architecture that chart Dublin's history.

Christchurch Cathedral. This is one of the oldest buildings in Dublin and, along with nearby Dublin Castle, forms the core of the oldest part of the city. The church traces its origins back to about 1030. Since the sixteenth century it has been under the auspices of the Church of Ireland. Much of what is visible of the church today dates from renovations during the Victorian era. The famous bells of Christchurch have been a prominent feature of Dublin's soundscape down through the centuries. (*Courtesy of the National Library of Ireland*)

Grattan Bridge and Ormond Quay church, 1890s. The handsome Ormond Quay Presbyterian church takes pride of place in this photograph. Built in 1847, very little remains of the church today, with only the ground floor façade still visible. The rest of it has become a generic office building. Grattan Bridge in the configuration shown dates from 1872, although there has been a bridge of some sort at this point since the 1600s.

(*Originally published in John F. Finnerty,* Ireland in Pictures (*J. S. Hyland & Co., 1898*))

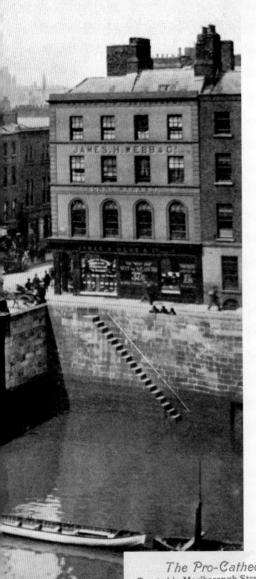

Below: **St Mary's, Marlborough Street.** St Mary's was consecrated in 1825. It was known as the Catholic Pro-Cathedral, essentially the acting cathedral, because Christ Church, despite being a Church of Ireland-run institution for many centuries, is still considered to be Dublin's official Catholic cathedral, having been designated as such by a pope in the twelfth century. The construction of St Mary's represented the regaining of the Catholic Church's status in Dublin after centuries of Penal Laws had stymied its ability to operate.
(*Courtesy of the Ken Finlay Collection*)

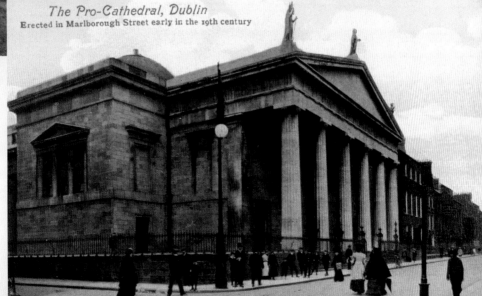

The Pro-Cathedral, Dublin
Erected in Marlborough Street early in the 19th century

St Patrick's Cathedral, Dublin, 1890s. With its origins in the twelfth century, St Patrick's is Ireland's largest church and since 1871 has served as the national church for the Church of Ireland (Anglican) congregation. Its famous spire was designed by George Semple and added to the building in 1749. The church was extensively reconstructed during the 1860s with funds from the Guinness family. (*Courtesy of the Library of Congress, LC-DIG-ppmsc-09874*)

Below: **St Patrick's Cathedral from St Patrick's Park.** St Patrick's Park, adjacent to the Cathedral was officially opened in 1902. It was largely the work of Lord Ardilaun and Lord Iveagh, two scions of the Guinness family who wielded patrician clout in their zeal for municipal improvement. Creating the park required the acquisition and levelling of numerous tenements.

(*Courtesy of the Ken Finlay Collection*)

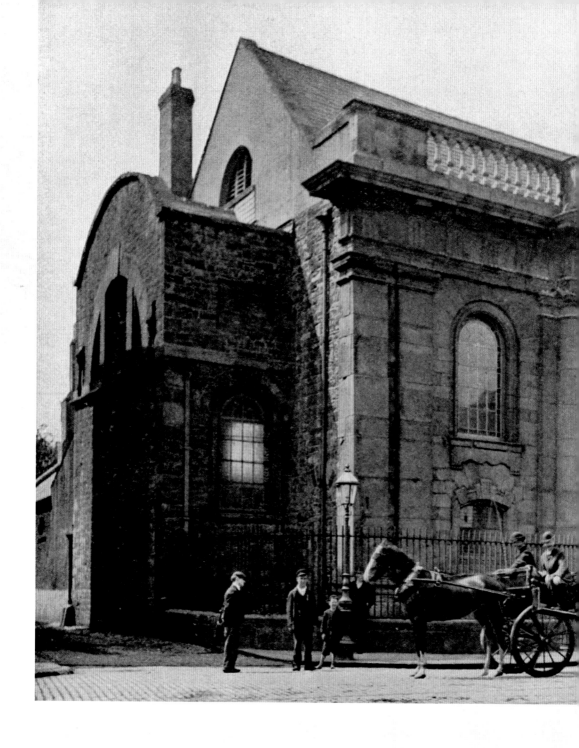

St Catherine's, Thomas Street, 1890s. The first church on this site was built in the twelfth century, though the building seen in this photograph dates from the 1760s. The church stands on the route of what was once known as the Slí Mhór, an ancient road that connected Dublin to Ireland's west. St Catherine's plays a significant part

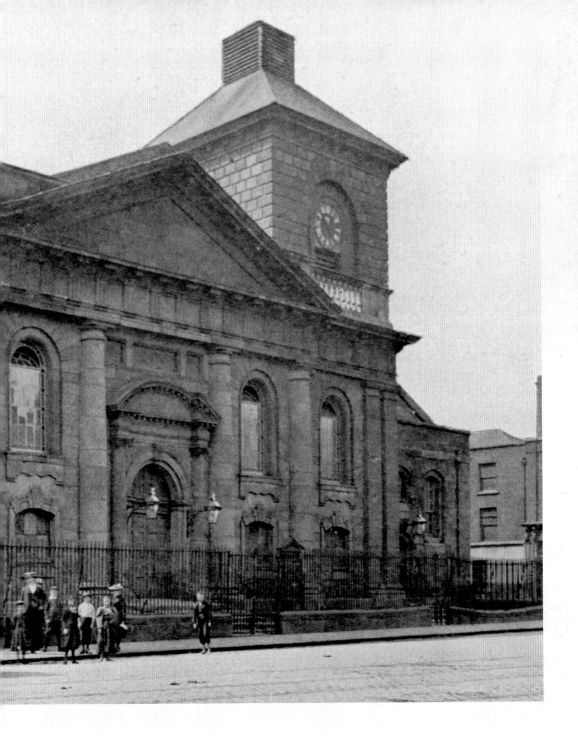

in Irish republican history, as it was here in 1803 that Robert Emmet was executed after his botched revolution. At the time this photograph was taken the church stood a stone's throw from some of the worst slums in Northern Europe.

(*Originally published in John F. Finnerty,* Ireland in Pictures (*J. S. Hyland & Co., 1898*))

Temple Street, early 1900s. This coloured postcard, dating from the early years of the twentieth century, has not one but two important North Dublin buildings in it. Construction on St George's church on Hardwicke Place began in 1802. The building was designed by Francis Johnston, perhaps best known as the architect of the GPO on Sackville Street. Temple Street Children's Hospital, to the right, first opened its doors in 1879 and continues to provide care for sick children to this day. (*Courtesy of the Ken Finlay Collection*)

Opposite: **Our Lady of Dolours Roman Catholic church, Dolphin's Barn, *c*. 1930s.** Built as a chapel-of-ease for a nearby parish in 1893, this church, along with several other recently constructed houses of worship, served the needs of an expanding city and suburban population. The name of the area, Dolphin's Barn, apparently originated with a local prominent family by the name of Dolphin or Dolphyn in the fourteenth century. The church is mislabelled in the postcard. (*Courtesy of the Ken Finlay Collection*)

Zion Road, Terenure

Above: Zion Road. This postcard is slightly inaccurate, as Zion Road is not actually in Terenure but in nearby Rathgar. On the right a young boy sits on a wall trying to get a look at something out of shot while his family stand patiently by. Save for a lone carriage the street is otherwise empty. The church in the distance is Zion Church of Ireland parish church.

(*Courtesy of the Ken Finlay Collection*)

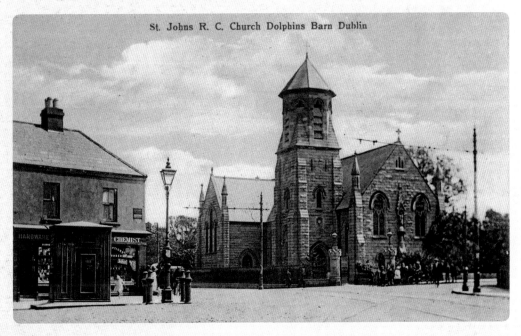

St. Johns R. C. Church Dolphins Barn Dublin

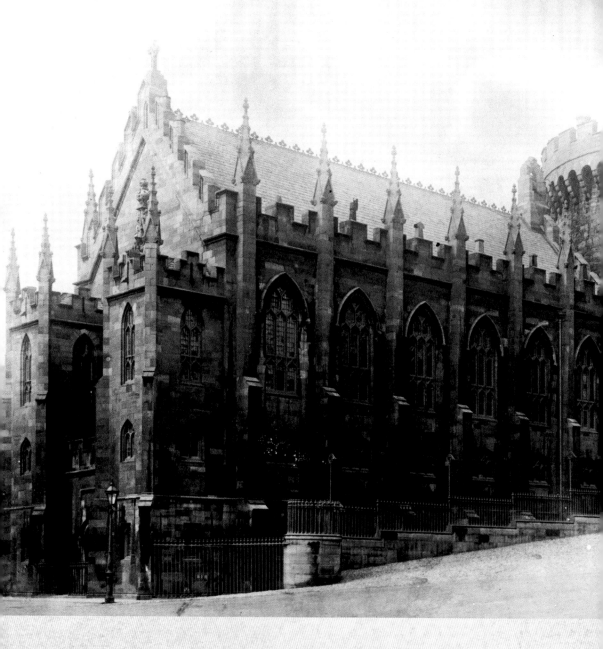

Dublin Castle and the Chapel Royal. These two views of the Dublin Castle present a scene that has barely changed in the intervening years, though the children frolicking on the grass in the postcard from *c.* 1905 must have long since grown up and passed on. At this time, the Francis Johnston-designed Chapel Royal was still the official Church of Ireland chapel of the household of the lord lieutenant. It ceased serving this function in 1922, when the role of lord lieutenant of Ireland was abolished. (*Courtesy of the Library of Congress, LC-DIG-npcc-19674 (above); the Ken Finlay Collection (right)*)

St Patrick's, Skerries, *c.* 1910. Skerries' main street has something of the aspect of a ghost town in this coloured postcard, with a lone woman walking up what is accurately called Church Street. The church in question is St Patrick's Roman Catholic church with its handsome belfry. Although the church was replaced in the 1930s, the belfry remains.
(*Courtesy of the Ken Finlay Collection*)

The Convent, Skerries, *c.* 1910. Of course churches and chapels are not the only type of religious buildings. This impressive-looking convent opened in 1883 and was run by the Holy Faith Sisters, who came to the town in 1875. The order provided instruction for adult learners as well as school-age children. The building stands in marked contrast to the humble cottages to the left.
(*Courtesy of the Ken Finlay Collection*)

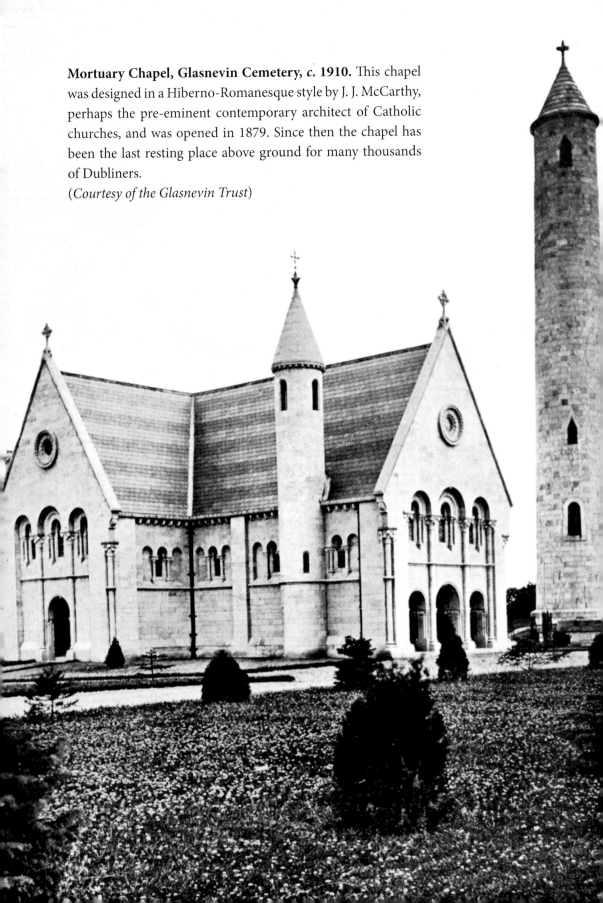

Mortuary Chapel, Glasnevin Cemetery, *c.* **1910.** This chapel was designed in a Hiberno-Romanesque style by J. J. McCarthy, perhaps the pre-eminent contemporary architect of Catholic churches, and was opened in 1879. Since then the chapel has been the last resting place above ground for many thousands of Dubliners.

(Courtesy of the Glasnevin Trust)

***Above and opposite*: Catholic Emancipation centenary celebrations.** In 1929 the nascent Free State saw perhaps its biggest public event up until that time. The Catholic Church held various celebrations to mark the centenary of Catholic Emancipation, which culminated in a pontifical high mass attended by an estimated 300,000 people. The mass was followed by a procession to Watling Street Bridge that concluded with a Benediction (*opposite bottom*). The women, girls and boys above were gathered on Westland Row.

The Catholic Church had unprecedented power and influence in the new Irish Free State and pageantry such as that displayed in these postcards was a common occurrence. These public displays of Irish Catholicism reached their zenith during the Eucharistic Congress of 1932, and the Church's influence did not wane for many years to come.

(*Courtesy of the Ken Finlay Collection*)

150

151

EUCHARISTIC CONGRESS, DUBLIN, 1932. Round Tower in College Green

Round Tower, College Green. This replica medieval round tower was temporarily erected on College Green for the benefit of international visitors to the city during the Eucharistic Congress of 1932. It was the most striking of a whole series of decorations that graced the city's streets during the congress. The successful running of the event was so important to the government of the day that they passed the Eucharistic Congress (Miscellaneous Provisions) Act, 1932, to facilitate preparations for the huge influx of visitors for the five-day event.
(*Courtesy of the Ken Finlay Collection*)

DUBLIN ON THE MOVE

In the late nineteenth and early twentieth centuries most people did not have their own vehicles. Cars were scarce even in the cities, and people relied on public transport to move around. Over time the type of transport changed, from horse-drawn carriages and omnibuses, to trams and then motorised buses. For longer trips there were trains and boats, and it was not until the 1930s that flying became an option for the public, although initially, only for the well-to-do.

Westmoreland Street, c. 1865. There is a lot going on here, in one of the earliest photographs in this collection. Taken at the corner of Westmoreland Street and College Street, the old, narrow Carlisle Bridge can just be made out in the background. Note the lack of trams, not fully implemented on Dublin's streets until 1872, with the horse-drawn omnibus in the foreground being the state-of-the-art city public transport of this time. Behind the omnibus is the statue of the great bard, Thomas Moore. Erected in 1857, it remains in situ to this day. Eagle-eyed readers may also notice the flock of sheep being herded in the background near the bridge. (*Courtesy of the National Library of Ireland*)

Grafton Street, *c.* 1870. This image gives a glimpse of Grafton Street's bustle in about 1870. Horse-drawn conveyances still held primacy and both men and women's fashions clearly differ from subsequent decades. Note the presence of the Dublin School of Photography at No. 79; this building (along with No. 78 next door) later became the home of Bewley's Oriental Café, a local signature building to this day. The street was not pedestrianised until 1982.

(*Courtesy of the National Library of Ireland*)

North-eastern corner of St Stephen's Green, *c.* 1890. The presence of the man with the Penny Farthing, an enduring symbol of the era, sealed the deal on this image's inclusion in this collection. The Penny Farthing was not a particularly safe means of transport, with a high risk of accident if the front wheel struck an obstacle. It was only with the invention of the safety bicycle and pneumatic tyres in the 1880s that cycling became a popular means of transport.
(*Courtesy of the National Library of Ireland*)

College Green and Dame Street, 1890s. This photograph was taken from an upstairs window in Trinity College. While affording a splendid view of the Bank of Ireland building, it also shows off the work of the Wide Streets Commission. The commission was set up in 1757, and in the 1770s it undertook to widen Dame Street,

an improvement that took many years to complete but is clearly in evidence in this photograph. Another feature worth noting is that the trams, along with all the other vehicles in this image, were still horse-drawn at this juncture.
(*Originally published in John F. Finnerty,* Ireland in Pictures *(J. S. Hyland & Co., 1898)*)

Kingsbridge Terminus, *c.* 1890. Named after nearby Kings Bridge, this train station opened in August 1846. The ornate building was designed by English architect Sancton Wood at the behest of the Great Western and Southern Railway Company (GWSR). The terminus served as the firm's headquarters. Since its completion the station has played an integral role in Dublin and Ireland's transport infrastructure, and continues in that function to this day, being a hub for railway services from Cork, Galway, Limerick, Waterford and elsewhere. In 1966 it was renamed Heuston Station, after Seán Heuston, one of the executed leaders of the Easter Rising, who had worked for the GWSR.

(*Courtesy of the National Library of Ireland*)

KINGSBRIDGE TERMINUS. 664!.W.L.

Inset: A Wills's cigarette card showing a Mogul-type goods locomotive of the Dublin and South Eastern Railway, which ran between Dublin and Wexford.
(*Courtesy of Mercier Archive*)

Passenger train, Kingsbridge Station, 1890s. Even with a city as patently fantastic as Dublin, it is sometimes necessary to leave. This photograph was taken at what looks to be Kingsbridge Station. A rail passenger leaving Dublin in the 1890s had access to many more towns and villages than the modern-day rail traveller does. This is because many of the lines that once criss-crossed the country were shut down during the twentieth century.

(Originally published in John F. Finnerty, Ireland in Pictures *(J. S. Hyland & Co., 1898))*

Queen Victoria. Of course, if you wanted to travel in style at this time, it was hard to beat the open-top carriage with its magnificent team of four horses and mounted escort used by Queen Victoria. This photograph was taken during Queen Victoria's final visit to Ireland, which occurred in 1900, not long before she passed on. She had visited Ireland a number of times before, perhaps most controversially in 1849 while the Great Famine still ravaged the country. In the photograph the carriage is passing Findlater's Mountjoy Brewery, which produced various stouts, ales and porters. Founded in 1852 and located on Russell Street just off the North Circular Road, the brewery remained in business until 1956.

(*Courtesy of the Fingal Local Studies Collection*)

Lawrence, Publisher, Dublin.

LARRY DOOLAN.

My name is Larry Doolan, I'm a native of the soil,
   If you want a day's 'divarshin' I'll dhrive you out in style,
My car is painted red and green, and on the well a star,
   And the pride of Dublin City is my 'Irish Jaunting Car'!

Larry Doolan postcard. This twee postcard reprints a verse from a song called 'The Irish Jaunting Car' penned by Valentine Vousden, which was immensely popular from the 1850s on. In another verse, the song mentions Queen Victoria's trip in a jaunting car during her visit to Ireland in 1849. Jaunting cars, light horse-drawn vehicles designed for sightseeing, are still to be seen in tourist spots around Ireland to this day.

(*Courtesy of the Ken Finlay Collection*)

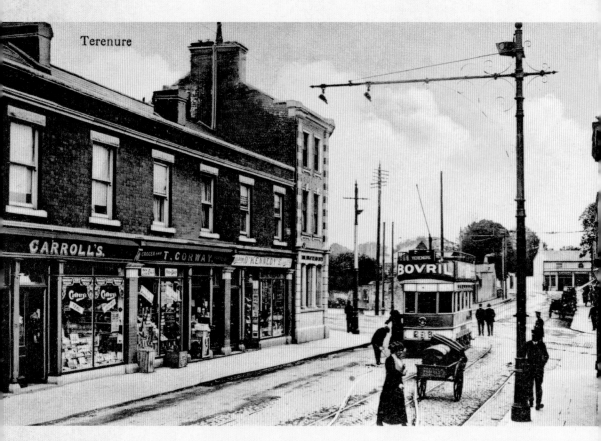

Terenure

Terenure, 1905. This photograph was taken on Terenure Road East facing towards Terenure Cross, which was a terminus for the trams. Tramlines began being laid in the early 1870s and for many years the trams were horse drawn. Electrification commenced in 1896, and by 1901 all the trams in Dublin were powered by electricity. Tram 288, pictured, appears to be in a spot of bother, though it is hard to make out what the workman is doing in front of it to remedy the situation. At its peak in 1911 the Dublin tram system had 330 operational trams that ran on over 60 miles (96 km) of track.

(*Courtesy of the Ken Finlay Collection*)

Opposite: **Tram to Howth Summit,** *c*. **1905.** The Hill of Howth Tramway ran from 1901 until 1959 and carried people from Sutton Railway Station, via the summit of the Hill of Howth, to Howth Railway Station. The single-track line is still fondly recalled by locals of a certain age.

(*Courtesy of the Fingal Local Studies Collection*)

Tram at Phoenix Park, early 1900s. Many a world-weary Edwardian Dubliner must have ridden the tram away from the city with its noise, smog and crowds, and alighted at Parkgate Street to go on a pleasant ramble in Phoenix Park. Perhaps they fed the deer, or maybe they deliberately got a little bit lost in the forest primeval. (*Courtesy of the Ken Finlay Collection*)

Motor car on St Stephen's Green, July 1903. When J. J. Clarke took this photograph, motorcars were still a novelty on the streets of Dublin, hence the crowd of onlookers. This Panhard 20 hp was probably brought to Ireland by a continental visitor attending the Gordon Bennett Race in Athy, Co. Kildare, and the Phoenix Park Speed Trials. In the wake of these two showcase events, ownership of motor cars in Ireland took off. Note also the two men with bicycles, which had become an increasingly popular conveyance.

(*Courtesy of the National Library of Ireland*)

An Rothar advertisement, 1910. A sign of the popularity of bicycles among all classes is this advertisement which appeared in a 1910 Abbey Theatre programme. It also reflects two related trends in Irish life at the time. It touts a 'buy Irish' philosophy which was popular in nationalist circles and the business' name at least pays lip service to the Gaelic revival, then reaching its zenith in Dublin city.
(*Author's collection*)

"THE PLAY IS THE THING"

Agreed, but after the play and in the intervals you will allow us to introduce—

"The Man at the 'Wheel'"
84 CAMDEN STREET,
DUBLIN.

An Rotar (The Wheel) is the only exclusively Irish Cycle Depot. The largest stock of Pierce and Lucania cycles in Ireland or out of it is carried at "The Wheel."

Irish and Best

We claim for the Pierce and Lucania cycles that they are superior to any foreign make whilst no dearer in price, and we put it to you as a business proposition that the least you should do before investing in a new mount is

"Speak to the Man at the 'Wheel'"

Note only address—84 CAMDEN ST.

Panhard and Napier cars, 1902. In 1901 Mr Charles Wisdom Hely, a stationer on Dame Street, bought a 7 hp Panhard in which he managed to cover 10,000 miles very quickly. In 1902 he ordered a 16 hp Napier and gave the Panhard to his daughter Violet, who was just thirteen at the time. She is recorded as driving it over the Wicklow mountain passes. Both can be seen here in their respective cars. (*Courtesy of the RIAC Archive*)

John Hutton and Sons Motor Works, *c*. 1901. John Hutton and Sons was established in Dublin in 1779 as a coachbuilding company. With the growing interest in motorised transport at the end of the nineteenth century, the company diversified, and their premises in Summerhill, shown here, became a motor repair depot for Daimler cars.

(*Courtesy of the RIAC Archive*)

O'Connell Bridge, *c.* 1911.
This image was taken from a glass lantern slide. Due to the decorations around Sackville Street and on the bridge, I suspect this photograph was taken at the time of King George V and Queen Mary's visit to Dublin. This royal visit, the third in a dozen years by a reigning British monarch, was to be the last one for a century. The Dalkey-bound tram at the centre advertises O'Mara's Limerick Bacon and Hams. (*Courtesy of the Ken Finlay Collection*)

Isle of Man boat, *c.* 1920s. This crowd, which had gathered to see off the boat to the Isle of Man, clearly illustrates the shift in fashions post-First World War. The cut of clothes and hats seems less formal than in the pre-war years. Most of the ladies photographed are wearing cloche hats, a look associated with the international flapper style of the roaring twenties and intermittently back in fashion ever since. (*Courtesy of the Ken Finlay Collection*)

Westmoreland St., Dublin. [Photo Lafeyette]

Westmoreland Street. As can be seen in this snapshot of *c.* 1920s central Dublin, the motor car had become more commonplace. Many men who served during the First World War learned to drive, and this helped spur demand in the post-war years. The tram advertises Lamb Brothers Jams, which had a factory in Inchicore and farms at Donabate and Rathfarnham.
(*Courtesy of the Ken Finlay Collection*)

Overleaf: **Dublin transport map, 1922–23.** This beautiful map shows the state of public transportation in the city on the cusp of a great change. The tramlines illustrated were entirely replaced by motorised buses by 1949, as buses were seen as more flexible and economical than trams. The city centre remained bereft of trams until the opening of the Luas light railway in 2004.
(*Courtesy of the Civics Institute of Ireland*)

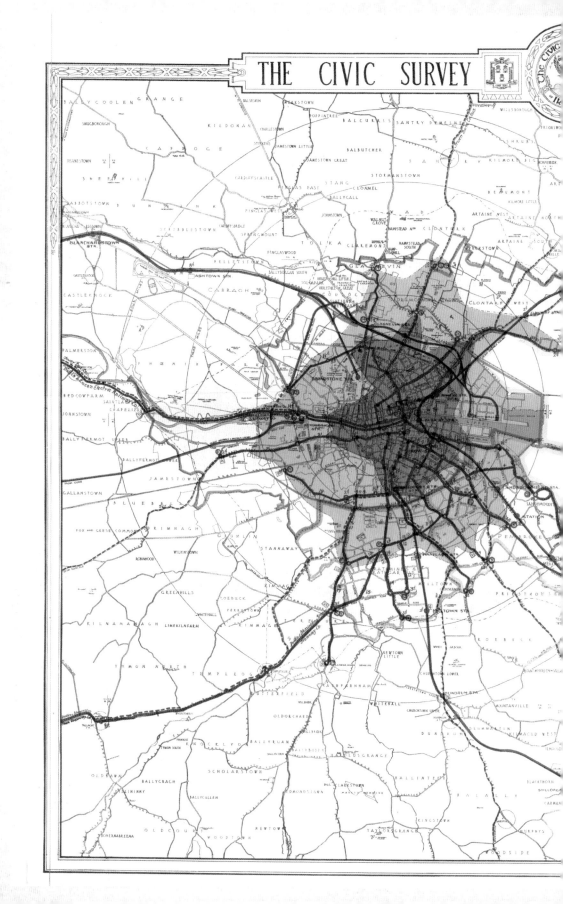

DUBLIN AND ENVIRONS

DVBLIN BAY

College Green, *c.* 1930. Trams, horse-drawn carriages, motor cars, lorries, pedestrians and cyclists are all present in this busy scene, but the proliferation of mechanised transport is notable. By this time Dublin trams had top covers which must have been a boon for commuters in a city not unfamiliar with rain. The last city centre tram was decommissioned in 1949, ultimately supplanted by the bus.
(*Courtesy of the National Library of Ireland*)

DUBLIN'S MONUMENTS

Anyone who knows Dublin will be aware of the numerous statues and monuments that are dotted around the city, sometimes obvious, sometimes hidden away. The following collection gives a selection of those that still exist and others that have disappeared forever.

(*Image courtesy of the National Library of Ireland*)

Nelson's Pillar. This postcard of Nelson's Pillar appears to be from the 1930s, although it may be from a bit later. Nelson's Pillar was a defining feature of Sackville/O'Connell Street from 1809 until it was blown up in 1966 by Irish republicans. The viewing platform atop the pillar afforded views across the city. By accident or, one suspects, design, a sign for Noblett's Confectioners appears on the bottom left of the postcard. Noblett's had several popular stores, one being on North Earl Street and another being at the St Stephen's Green end of Grafton Street.
(*Courtesy of the Ken Finlay Collection*)

View from the top of Nelson's Pillar, c. 1921. As the saying goes, all human life is here. This photograph was taken from the viewing platform of Nelson's Pillar and looks down at the junction of Henry Street and Sackville Street. A large crowd has congregated and appears to have formed a queue, but history has not recorded what the occasion was. There are at least two policemen in the scene and a number of other individuals who appear to be in uniform, perhaps soldiers.
(*Courtesy of the National Library of Ireland*)

Purcell's Tobacconists advertisement, 1909. Another humorous ad from the pages of *The Lepracaun*. Nelson's Pillar was a mainstay of Dublin print advertisements down the years and many Dubliners navigated the streets of the city with reference to the landmark, as it marked the terminus of many of the trams.

Queen Victoria Statue, Leinster House, *c.* 1908. This statue was erected in memory of Queen Victoria in 1908, the work of John Hughes, RHA, a renowned Dublin sculptor. It was none too popular in post-independence Dublin and was removed from the grounds of Leinster House in 1948. Having spent many years in storage at Kilmainham Hospital and elsewhere, it was given as a gift to Australia in the 1980s. The statue can now be found outside the Queen Victoria Building in Sydney. (*Courtesy of the Ken Finlay Collection*)

Phoenix Park postcard, *c.* 1920s. This postcard depicts in stylised fashion the Phoenix Column in Phoenix Park. It consists of a phoenix rising from flames on top of a Corinthian column and was erected by the 4th Earl of Chesterfield in 1747. The earl also opened the park to the public. (*Courtesy of the Ken Finlay Collection*)

Wellington Testimonial, *c.* 1890. This massive obelisk was constructed in Phoenix Park in honour of Arthur Wellesley, 1st Duke of Wellington, one of the heroes of the Napoleonic Wars. Standing at sixty-two metres tall, the structure had a difficult genesis. It was originally meant to be built in Merrion Square, but objections from residents scuppered that idea. Although the foundation stone was laid in 1817, due to a shortage of funds it was not completed until 1861. Wellesley's

supposed distaste for Ireland, encapsulated in the quote still sometimes attributed to him – 'If a gentleman happens to be born in a stable, it does not follow that he should be called a horse' – seems to have been at the very least exaggerated by his political rival, Daniel O'Connell, who may even be the progenitor of the quote. (*Courtesy of the Library of Congress, LC-DIG-ppmsc-009878*)

Field Marshal Gough Statue, Phoenix Park. Another of Phoenix Park's monuments is to a native of Woodstown, Co. Limerick. Gough had been decorated for his involvement in military campaigns against, among others, the Marathas, the Sikhs and the French. Winston Churchill, a childhood resident of Dublin, recalled the unveiling of the John Foley-designed statue in 1878 as his earliest memory. Like other statues that were seen to represent British rule, it was vandalised several times, most notably on Christmas Eve 1944, when parties unknown decapitated it. The head was later retrieved from the Liffey and the statue continued to lie in situ until 1957 when, after a dynamite attack, city officials felt it best to mothball it. The 1957 dynamite attack inspired a wonderful bawdy poem by Dubliner Vince Caprani, which is sadly a little too rude to reproduce here!
(*Courtesy of the Ken Finlay Collection*)

186

John Gray. This image, from around the turn of the twentieth century, shows the white statue on Sackville Street of John Gray, who helped to bring a fresh water supply infrastructure to Dublin. His work was so appreciated by Dubliners that they built a statue in his honour shortly after his death in 1875. The French-style building to the left of the GPO was the Hotel Metropole, which was largely destroyed during Easter Week, 1916.

(*Courtesy of the Ken Finlay Collection*)

O'Connell Statue. After eighteen years of work, John Henry Foley's statue of Daniel O'Connell was unveiled in 1882. Such is the statue's symbolic significance that in 1969, when the Troubles were kicking off, loyalist paramilitaries attempted to blow it up, but failed.

(*Courtesy of the Ken Finlay Collection*)

GRATTAN STATUE, COLLEGE GREEN, DUBLIN 01863

Grattan Statue, College Green. This bronze statue was erected to the memory of Henry Grattan, an Irish politician and member of the Irish House of Commons. Grattan helped win legislative independence for Ireland in 1782 and headed opposition to the 1800 Act of Union. The lamps around the statue show that this image was taken in the late nineteenth century. Grattan Bridge, which crosses the Liffey between Parliament Street and Capel Street, is also named in his honour.

In the misty background King Billy faces away down Dame Street. Nowadays King Billy is long gone, having been removed following an explosion in 1928, and Grattan is shrouded by trees which reduce somewhat the statue's impact.
(*Courtesy of the Ken Finlay Collection*)

DUBLIN'S SUBURBS

Much of what makes up the suburbs of Dublin city today, was originally a series of villages that surrounded the city but were not in fact part of it. These areas have retained not only their names but also their distinct identities, despite having been swallowed up by the modern expansion of the city.

Killiney and Dalkey, 1890s. This view looks north-east, taking in Killiney, Killiney Hill and nearby Dalkey. The obelisk on the summit of Killiney Hill can clearly be seen as well as some of the area's salubrious homes, such as Victoria Castle, the castellated mansion built in 1840, nowadays dubbed Manderley Castle and owned by the singer Enya. These two villages, along with nearby Dún Laoghaire, are sometimes referred to as Bel Eire by latter-day wags due to the preponderance of mansions and celebrity residents.

(Courtesy of the Library of Congress, LC-DIG-ppmsc-09882)

Below: **Killiney Bay from Obelisk Park.** This view looks south along the majestic Vale of Shanganagh towards Bray, just over the Wicklow border. It also affords a clear view of Victoria Castle.

(*Courtesy of the Ken Finlay Collection*)

Main Street, Tallaght, early 1900s. As much as Tallaght has been transformed in recent decades, with a huge influx of people and massive commercial, residential and industrial development, this street today looks essentially the same as it did all those years ago. For all the vast change that has swept over Dublin in the past hundred and more years, there are many lasting continuities of place and character. (*Courtesy of the National Library of Ireland*)

Idrone Terrace, Blackrock, *c.* 1900. At the time this photograph was taken, this was a very fashionable address, with an unimpeded view of Dublin Bay, and indeed properties on the terrace still fetch enviable prices today. The urban middle class from the city proper flocked to Blackrock and its environs after the completion of the Dublin and Kingstown Railway in 1834, Ireland's first railway. The coming of the railways allowed for the gradual but inexorable suburbanisation of Dublin, with once discrete villages being absorbed into the city's far-reaching sprawl.
(*Courtesy of the Ken Finlay Collection*)

Opposite: **Ballsbridge.** Ballsbridge, built in 1791, spans the Dodder River in the area once commonly known as Pembroke, though nowadays almost universally referred to as Ballsbridge. For many years this area has been home to some of the most exclusive residences in the city as well as the grounds of the Royal Dublin Society.
(*Courtesy of the Ken Finlay Collection*)

Rathgar showing Christ Church (Presbyterian), Dublin

Above: **Rathgar, *c*. 1905.** This postcard depicts the commercial heart of this salubrious suburban village and shows the various methods of conveyance used at that time. In the background is the steeple of Christ Church Presbyterian church, the foundation stone of which was laid in 1860. It opened in February 1862.
(*Courtesy of the Ken Finlay Collection*)

Ballsbridge

Rathmines Junction, August 1911. Rathmines has a long and colourful history and has been one of the pre-eminent suburbs of Dublin for many years. From the mid-nineteenth century on, many well-to-do city dwellers migrated out to the village in a bid to avoid the overcrowding and poverty that was becoming endemic in the inner city. This photograph shows the array of prosperous-looking small businesses that surrounded the junction.

(*Courtesy of the National Library of Ireland*)

Round Tower, Clondalkin.
The Round Tower in Clondalkin is an enduring icon and focal point of the town. At the time this postcard was created, Clondalkin was a village, with a population numbering in the low hundreds. Like Lucan, Blanchardstown, Tallaght and other villages around the city, Clondalkin has grown into a substantial and sprawling settlement in the years since.
(*Courtesy of the Ken Finlay Collection*)

Lucan from the South, Co. Dublin

Lucan from the south, 1913. The children in the field in the foreground appear to be having lessons outdoors or are otherwise enjoying the pleasant weather. As with many villages in County Dublin away from the city proper, the character of Lucan has changed immensely due to suburbanisation and sprawl. The spire seen in the distance is that of St Andrew's Church of Ireland church.
(*Courtesy of the Ken Finlay Collection*)

Opposite: **Stillorgan Village, *c.* 1905.** As surely as the coming of the railways altered the character of towns and villages along their routes during the Victorian era, so too did the tramways, motorised buses and private motor cars of a later epoch. These advances made it easier for people to abandon the overcrowded city and settle in pastures new. As with most other villages that once surrounded the city, Stillorgan has in recent times become a commuter suburb. Most suburban towns around the city still have an area referred to locally as 'the village'.
(*Courtesy of the Ken Finlay Collection*)

North Circular Road at Hanlon's Corner. Moving to the north side of the city now, this photograph provides a stunning view of the terraced three-storey houses along the North Circular Road, with the Wellington Testimonial in the background. As in other parts of the city, this area has changed quite fundamentally in socioeconomic terms. Whereas middle- and upper-middle-class families occupied these houses when this photograph was taken, they are now typically subdivided into flats for people of more modest means.
(*Courtesy of the National Library of Ireland*)

TO CITY
WAIT HERE
FOR CAR

Doyle's Corner, Phibsboro, *c.* 1915. Looking west towards St Peter's church, this scene has changed remarkably little in the intervening century, the main difference being the presence of the tram tracks and the absence of traffic lights at the junction. The Bohemian Bar on the right in particular looks much the same as it did. The policeman appears poised to stop the oncoming vehicle. (*Courtesy of the National Library of Ireland*)

Main Street, Swords, *c.* **1900s.** Nowadays a sprawling commuter town, Swords was a rural village when this photograph was taken, with many people in the district employed as farm labourers. The village was the scene of a riot during the 1913 Dublin Lock-out, when 300 striking labourers briefly ran the local constabulary out of town.
(*Courtesy of the National Library of Ireland*)

Howth and Ireland's Eye, 1890s. Then, as now, Howth was primarily a fishing village, as well as being a popular seaside resort. Ireland's Eye is an uninhabited island a short distance from Howth Harbour, which was the scene of a crime that shocked mid-nineteenth-century Dublin society. In September 1852 Sarah Kirwan died while on a day trip to the island. Her husband, William Burke Kirwan, was

charged with and convicted of her murder. Isaac Butt, who later became a leading light in the Irish Home Rule movement, led Kirwan's defence. The privately owned Lambay Island can also be seen in the distance.

(*Courtesy of the Library of Congress, LC-DIG-ppmsc-09883*)

Baily Lighthouse, Howth. The Baily Lighthouse, misspelled on this postcard as Bailey, has stood at the south-eastern end of Howth since 1814. It is the latest in a series of lighthouses erected in the area since the 1660s. The Baily is maintained by the Commissioners of Irish Lights.
(*Courtesy of the Ken Finlay Collection*)

Fairview Corner, early 1900s. An interesting feature in this postcard is that the store in the centre bears the name Edge. Unfortunately, it's not clear what type of business it was then, but the Edge name is still attached to the premises, and it's being run as a hardware store more than a century later. So long has the Edge family's tenure been at this locale that the area is known as Edge's Corner by locals.
(*Courtesy of the Ken Finlay Collection*)

Chapel Street, Malahide, *c.* 1918. This postcard, produced by the Scottish firm, Valentine & Sons, shows a street scene in Malahide all but unrecognisable today. The thatched cottages depicted were the predominant type of dwelling in north Dublin at the time. The vast majority of these cottages have long since been replaced with more modern dwellings. Only two examples remain in Malahide at the present time. (*Courtesy of the Fingal Local Studies Collection*)

The Diamond, Malahide. When the Dublin to Belfast railway line was laid in the 1840s, Malahide became a popular residential area for well-heeled city folk seeking to escape the city centre. However, it was not until well into the twentieth century that this picturesque seaside village developed into a major town. (*Courtesy of the Ken Finlay Collection*)

Malahide Castle. This castle has been an iconic part of the Malahide landscape for centuries. Originally built in the twelfth century by Richard Talbot, who came to Ireland with Henry II, the castle was owned by that family until it was sold to the Irish state in 1975. The towers were added in 1765.
(*Courtesy of the National Library of Ireland*)

The Strawberry Beds, *c.* **1900s.** The Strawberry Beds run along the northern bank of the Liffey between Chapelizod and Lucan. Not surprisingly they get their name from the strawberries that once grew in abundance there and were sold by roadside traders. For many years the Strawberry Beds have offered respite from the noise and crowds of the city a few short miles away, and the area was popular with honeymooners before more exotic locations were accessible. It seems that in the latter years of the nineteenth century, enterprising men with horses and traps charged 3 pence to ferry day-trippers from Carlisle Bridge to the Beds and back again.
(*Courtesy of the National Library of Ireland and the Ken Finlay Collection (postcard)*)

ICONIC
DUBLIN

There are some buildings in Dublin that everyone can recognise at a glance, not just in Ireland, but around the world – the GPO, Trinity College, the old Parliament House (now the Bank of Ireland) on College Green. However, not all the iconic sights of Dublin fall under the category of buildings. Moreover, there are a few buildings included in this section that may not be well known, due to their neglect or their loss, but they deserve not to be forgotten all the same.

OBEDIENTIA ‖‖ FELICITAS

CIVIUM URBIS

DUBLIN.

HERALDIC SERIES.

Dublin's coat of arms, *c*. 1910. Observant visitors and locals alike may have noticed this coat of arms emblazoned on bins and lamp posts throughout the city centre. The motto *Obedientia civium, urbis felicitas* is Latin and roughly translates as 'An obedient population makes for a happy city'. It dates back at least 400 years, although its ultimate origins are lost to time. Joyce riffed on the motto throughout his cryptic final novel *Finnegans Wake*. In more recent times there have been calls from some quarters for the motto to be replaced with something that reflects more modern attitudes, although it seems unlikely it ever will be.
(*Courtesy of the Ken Finlay Collection*)

Government Buildings, Upper Merrion Street, *c.* 1930. Built as the new head-quarters of the Royal College of Science for Ireland, this building was the last major public building undertaken in Dublin under British rule. Having been completed in 1911, the building would later serve as the home of the short-lived Parliament of Southern Ireland. In 1922 the Free State government took over some of the building as office space and various government departments including the Department of the Taoiseach would share the building with the Royal College of Science until 1991. Thereafter it was refurbished and given over wholly to government business. (*Courtesy of the Ken Finlay Collection*)

Leinster House. Commissioned by James Fitzgerald, the Earl of Kildare, and built between 1745 and 1747, Leinster House was originally known as Kildare House. The name was changed when Fitzgerald became Duke of Leinster in 1776. Designed by the German architect Richard Cassels, it has been suggested that the White House in Washington was modelled on this building. In 1815 the mansion was sold to the Royal Dublin Society and the building was acquired by the State in 1924. The National Library to the left of the image was established with the passing of the Dublin Science and Art Museum Act of 1877, which also allowed for the creation of the very similar National Museum opposite it. The purpose-built building was designed by Cork architect Thomas Deane and was finished in 1890.
(Courtesy of the National Library of Ireland)

The National Museum, Dublin.

DUBLIN MUSEUM.

Opposite: **The National Museum, *c*. 1910.** The museum was established in 1877 and built in tandem with the National Library on ground adjacent to Leinster House, being completed in 1890. It originally housed the collection of the Royal Dublin Society Museum and was later bolstered with additions from the Royal Irish Academy and Trinity College. The building now houses the archaeology section of the museum's collection, with other premises housing other national treasures, including Collins Barracks (*below*). The museum's most famous piece is probably the Ardagh Chalice, an intricate eighth-century Christian artefact well known to the generations of bored school children who have been brought to see it!
(*Courtesy of the Ken Finlay Collection*)

Royal Barracks from South Quays, Dublin

Royal Barracks, *c*. 1910. Sitting in Arbour Hill on the north bank of the Liffey, these barracks were constructed in 1702 and were continuously garrisoned until 1997. After the abortive rising in 1798, the most prominent leader of the rising, Theobald Wolfe Tone, was held in the provost's prison within the barracks. There he was court-martialled and convicted of treason, but shortly before he was due to be executed, he took his own life. Originally known simply as the Barracks, they became the Royal Barracks in the early nineteenth century and Collins Barracks in 1922, shortly after the establishment of the Irish Free State. Since 1997 the barracks have been home to the Decorative Arts and History branch of the National Museum.
(*Courtesy of the Ken Finlay Collection*)

The GPO and Nelson's Pillar, Sackville Street. Of these two icons of Dublin, Nelson's Pillar was actually built first, with its formal opening ceremony held in October 1809. The GPO, purpose-built to replace its predecessor on College Green, was designed by Francis Johnston and opened for business on 6 January 1818, having been completed in less than four years.
(*Courtesy of the National Library of Ireland*)

G.P.O. & NELSON PILLAR. DUBLIN. Nº 1. W.L.

Dublin Castle. A fortification has stood on the site of Dublin Castle since Viking times, but the first stone castle there was commissioned by King John of England in 1204 and completed in 1230. Since then the site has been in continuous use, although little of the original castle remains. This photograph shows the Great Courtyard or Upper Castle Yard, which was completed in the mid-eighteenth century. To the left is Castle Hall and the Bedford Tower, with the Cork Hill gate on the far side of it, and on the right are the State Apartments.
(*Courtesy of the National Library of Ireland*)

The Four Courts, 1890s. Constructed between 1786 and 1802, the Four Courts derives its name from its original courts of Chancery, King's Bench, Exchequer and Common Pleas. Reform in the latter part of the nineteenth century abolished these courts, but the name stuck. This picture shows it in all its pristine pre-war glory. Having survived the 1916 Rising largely unscathed, the building sustained extensive damage during the Civil War, when anti-Treaty forces occupied it. Sadly, during the battle a huge swathe of Irish historical records at the Public Records Office was lost. (*Originally published in John F. Finnerty,* Ireland in Pictures *(J. S. Hyland & Co., 1898)*)

Below: **The Liffey and the Four Courts.** This coloured postcard from the early 1900s depicts two Dublin icons: the imposing Four Courts and the elementally splendid Liffey. Rising in the Wicklow Mountains, the river has been fundamental to the continued existence of Dublin as a city. For most of the city's existence the river was a major trade artery and to this day it supplies the majority of the city's drinking water. The river has also served as an inspiration for songs, poetry and prose, most famously in the character of Anna Livia Plurabelle in Joyce's *Finnegans Wake*.
(*Courtesy of the Ken Finlay Collection*)

The Liffey and Four Courts, Dublin

MANSION HOUSE. DUBLIN 4736. W L.

The Mansion House. Built between 1705 and 1710, this Queen Anne-style house has been the residence of the Lord Mayor of Dublin since 1715, making it the oldest mayoral residence still in use in Britain and Ireland. The building also hosted the first Dáil, in January 1919. (*Courtesy of the National Library of Ireland*)

The Long Room, Old Library, Trinity College, 1890s. This fantastic library was constructed between 1712 and 1732 and was significantly altered in the mid-1800s to accommodate its myriad tomes. The busts commemorate great men (and they're all men) of western thought and various grandees, both famous and obscure, of the college. This scene may well be the least changed of all presented in this book. (*Originally published in John F. Finnerty,* Ireland in Pictures *(J. S. Hyland & Co., 1898)*)

Opposite: **Trinity College and the Bank of Ireland building, c. 1905.** Trinity College and the Bank of Ireland represent perhaps the most recognisable icons of Dublin after the GPO, the Ha'penny Bridge and, of course, a pint of Guinness. Trinity College was established in 1592, during the reign of Queen Elizabeth I. The Bank of Ireland building is a relative newcomer, having been constructed in 1720 to house the Irish Parliament. (*Courtesy of the Ken Finlay Collection*)

Trinity College Dublin crest, early twentieth century. The inscription surrounding this version of Trinity's crest reads *Collegium Sanctae et Individuae Trinitatis Reginae Elizabethae juxta Dublin*, Latin for 'The College of the Holy and Undivided Trinity of Queen Elizabeth near Dublin' which is the college's full official name. The Bible is clasped here, while typically unclasped in later versions. In recent times the college has controversially spent €100,000 rebranding, with alterations made to the crest and the college's name that have raised the ire of many.

(*Courtesy of the Ken Finlay Collection*)

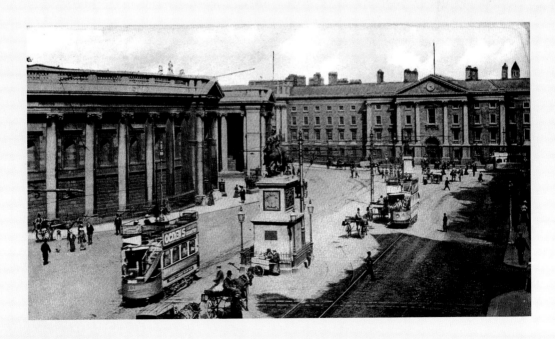

12043. - BANK OF IRELAND. DUBLIN.

Bank of Ireland, College Green, 1890s. This building was designed by Edward Lovett Pearce in the 1720s and constructed as Ireland's Houses of Parliament, hence its grandiose scale. James Gandon extended the building in the 1780s. When the Act of Union of 1800 made its original purpose redundant, it was taken over by the Bank of Ireland. The statues by Edward Smyth over what was the portico to the House of Lords symbolise wisdom, justice and liberty. This photograph was presumably taken early one bright morning as, save for a solitary spectator, no traffic is discernible on the usually bustling thoroughfare. (*Courtesy of the Library of Congress, LC-DIG-ppmsc-09873*)

Bank of Ireland, 1903. At first glance this unusual view of the bank looks like it was taken around Christmas time. However, the festive decorations adorning the building were to celebrate the visit of King Edward VII and Princess Alexandra to the city. Royal visits to the city in the years just before independence were met with huge crowds and garlands as well as vociferous protests by nationalists.
(*Courtesy of the Ken Finlay Collection*)

Hotel Metropole, Sackville Street, *c.* 1910. Located adjacent to the GPO, the Hotel Metropole began as four Georgian buildings, tied together to make the Prince of Wales Hotel. In the early 1890s the building was extensively remodelled in the style pictured. The building was irrevocably damaged during the fighting of Easter Week 1916. The Metropole lives on in a mention in Pete St John's elegiac 'The Rare Ould Times'.
(*Courtesy of the Ken Finlay Collection*)

Belcamp College, Balgriffin, *c.* 1920s. Belcamp Hall was designed in the 1770s for Sir Edward Newenham by James Hoban, the architect of the White House. The building became a boarding school in 1893, under the auspices of the Oblate Fathers, and operated until 2004, when it was sold to developers. In the intervening years the building has sadly gone to rack and ruin.
(*Courtesy of the Ken Finlay Collection*)

St John of God Hospital, Stillorgan, early 1900s. This hospital opened in 1882, specialising from the outset in providing care for people with mental illness. The hospital gets a mention in James Joyce's *Ulysses* and also plays a more extensive part, albeit in fictionalised form, in the works of Samuel Beckett.
(*Courtesy of the Ken Finlay Collection*)

Mater Misericordiae Hospital, Eccles Street. The Mater Hospital first opened its doors in 1861, and this elegant building was the work of John Bourke, a local Dublin architect. Bourke travelled extensively across Europe to view and learn from the top hospitals of the day when designing the Mater. Built by the Sisters of Mercy, the Mater was opened to care for the burgeoning poor of Dublin's inner city. (*Courtesy of the National Library of Ireland*)

Viceregal Lodge,Phoenix Park Dublin.

Viceregal Lodge, Phoenix Park. Nowadays called Áras an Uachtaráin, the Viceregal Lodge was built in the 1750s and served as a residence for lord lieutenants of Ireland from 1780 until 1922. For part of his childhood, while his grandfather served as lord lieutenant, Winston Churchill lived next door at the Little Lodge. In his later years he recalled fondly times spent in Phoenix Park as a boy. It has been suggested that the porticoes of the Viceregal Lodge inspired Irish architect James Hoban when designing the White House in Washington, but there is a certain amount of confusion about the matter.

(*Courtesy of the Ken Finlay Collection*)

Commander O. F. Quarters, Royal Hospital, Kilmainham, Dublin.

Royal Hospital, Kilmainham, early twentieth century. The Royal Hospital in Kilmainham is perhaps the finest building constructed in Dublin in the seventeenth century. The building was designed in the 1680s by William Robinson, surveyor general of Dublin, who was also responsible for designing those other enduring icons, St Michan's church and Marsh's Library. After housing retired veterans until 1927, it was then used by An Garda Síochána and later as a storage facility by the National Museum. It was refurbished in the 1980s and is now home to the Irish Museum of Modern Art. The expansive grounds of the hospital are used for concerts during the summer months.
(*Courtesy of the Ken Finlay Collection*)

Opposite: **Royal Irish Constabulary Barracks, Phoenix Park, *c*. 1910.** This building was purpose-built as the primary depot for the recruitment and training of the Irish constabulary and was completed in 1842. The RIC was an armed police force that covered Ireland outside Dublin city, with special divisions existing in Belfast and Derry. The building served its original function for about eighty years, until 1922, when the RIC was disbanded and replaced by the Civic Guards, later the Garda Síochána. This new police force of the Irish Free State took over the barracks and has occupied it ever since.
(*Courtesy of the Ken Finlay Collection*)

CITY HALL. DUBLIN. 1550. W.L.

City Hall. Designed by Thomas Cooley, this was originally the Royal Exchange, constructed specifically for the use of Dublin's merchant population between 1769 and 1779. In 1814 the balustrade at the front of the building collapsed, killing a number of people gathered outside. An iron railing was erected in its place, but in 1866 Dublin Corporation, which took over the building in 1851, accepted a design by Thomas Turner for a replacement stone balustrade more in keeping with the original. (*Courtesy of the National Library of Ireland*)

Kilmainham Gaol. Kilmainham Gaol is probably best known for being the scene of the executions of the leaders of the 1916 rebellion. Opened in 1796, it actually closed as a gaol in 1910, but was used to incarcerate political prisoners from 1916–24. More recently the gaol has seen use in a number of films and TV adaptations, including *The Wind that Shakes the Barley*, *Michael Collins* and the BBC programme *Ripper Street*. The iconic East Wing opened in 1862, and the photograph on the left was taken not long afterwards. Above is the front gate of the gaol.
(*Courtesy of Kilmainham Gaol Museum*)

The Custom House, 1908. Commissioned by John Beresford, Chief Revenue Commissioner, and designed by London architect James Gandon, the Custom House took ten years to build and was completed in 1791. Initially the headquarters of the Commissioners of Custom and Excise, by the beginning of the twentieth century its dominant role was as the seat of local government in Ireland. The building was attacked and burned by the IRA on 25 May 1921. Although restored following the burning, thousands of local government documents dating back centuries were destroyed in the blaze, a loss lamented by historians to this day. (*Courtesy of the Library of Congress, LC-USZ62-112333*)

St Stephen's Green, 1890s. From this vantage you can clearly see the contemporary cityscape along the western side of St Stephen's Green and beyond. Clearly identifiable landmarks include the Unitarian church dating from 1863 (*on the left*), the Royal College of Surgeons, completed in 1810, and in the distance the spire of St Patrick's Cathedral. (*Courtesy of the Library of Congress, LC-DIG-ppmsc-009877*)

Above: **St Stephen's Green at night.** A similar view to the one on the previous page, this differs in that it offers a slightly eerie night view. The moon and the lights in the windows give the illusion of lighting up when the postcard is held up to a light source. When presented with vistas such as this, it becomes easier to understand how Bram Stoker, who grew up on the square, came up with his Gothic horror classic *Dracula*. (*Courtesy of the Ken Finlay Collection*)

Merrion Square, Dublin

Daniel O'Connell and many other noted men have lived in this famous Square

Ha'penny Bridge and the Liffey quays, 1890s. For those familiar with this part of Dublin's quays, what's perhaps most notable is the absence of the Millennium Bridge, which these days offers fantastic views of the Ha'penny Bridge. Erected in 1816, the Ha'penny bridge (which is officially called the Liffey Bridge and originally was entitled the Wellington Bridge) gets its name from the toll that was paid to cross it. Tolls remained in place for over a hundred years. It seems that the toll men even tried to get Volunteers fighting during Easter Week 1916 to pay up! As can be seen in this photograph, the bridge was often festooned with advertisements, a practice which only ceased in the 1950s. Having been refurbished in 2001, the Ha'penny Bridge remains an enduring symbol of Dublin's fair city.

(*Originally published in John F. Finnerty,* Ireland in Pictures *(J. S. Hyland & Co., 1898)*)

Opposite: **Merrion Square from Leinster Lawn, *c*. 1905.** As the postcard notes, storied Merrion Square has been home to many players in the history of Ireland. With the completion of Leinster House, the Earl of Kildare's residence, in 1748, Dublin's hitherto less-developed southside became fashionable with the city's aristocratic elite. The well-to-do, previously ensconced on Rutland (now Parnell) and Mountjoy Squares, upped sticks for Merrion Square and other nearby fashionable addresses. Notable residents have included Henry Grattan, W. B. Yeats and Oscar Wilde, who has a colourful memorial statue dedicated to him on the square.

(*Courtesy of the Ken Finlay Collection*)

Prospect Cemetery—List of Charges.

LOCATION	SECTION	Charges for securing Exclusive Rights of Burial in Graves, Plots, Vaults, &c., in Perpetuity			Fees for Interment to be paid in addition to charges for securing Exclusive Right of Burial in Graves. Plots, Vaults, etc.	
		In Plot of 2 ft. by 8 ft.	In Plot of 4 ft. by 8 ft.	Any greater Quantity per superficial foot	Each Adult	Each Child under 12 yrs.
		£ s. d.	£ s. d.	£ s. d.	£ s. d.	£ s. d.
	Chapel Circle ..	...	32 0 0	1 0 0	1 10 0	1 0 0
	Curran's Square	...	15 0 0	0 12 6		
	O'Connell Circle	...	30 0 0	0 18 9	2 0 0	1 10 0
	No Plot less than 8 ft. long by 6 ft. wide to be disposed of, excepting where that quantity is not available.					
	SOUTH.					
NEW CHAPEL SECTION— Ground contiguous to New Chapel and the Tower. from Tc. 44 to the highest number on Kd., and from Hd. 1 to the highest number on Hf.	All Plots along the New Entrance Main Walk, and at rear of Vaults at the Tower, subject to Committee's permission ..	...	100 0 0	3 2 6		
	All Plots at Angles of Walks, other than the foregoing within the limits specified	...	64 0 0	2 0 0	3 0 0	2 0 0
	All Plots along Walks, the foregoing excepted, within the limits specified	...	48 0 0	1 10 0		
	All other Plots in from Walks	...	32 0 0	1 0 0		
	No Plot less than 8 ft. by 6 ft. to be disposed of, and suitable Monuments must be erected					
SOUTH SECTION— East of New Entrance. from V. to the highest number in Pc. inclusive.	All First or Border Plots along Walks	...	15 0 0	0 12 6	1 10 0	1 0 0
	No Plot less than 8 ft. by 6 ft. to be disposed of, excepting where that quantity is not available.					
	All Second Plots next Walks ..	...	10 0 0	0 8 4		
	All Third Plots next Walks ..	...	7 10 0	0 8 4		
	Fourth and all other Plots in from Walks	...	4 0 0	0 4 2	0 17 6	0 10 0
Pc. 1 to Kd. 41	First Plot next Walks	...	15 0 0	0 12 6	1 10 0	1 0 0
	Second Plots next Walks	...	10 0 0	0 8 4		
	Third Plots next Walks	...	7 10 0	0 8 4		
	Fourth and other Plots in from Walks	2 0 0	4 0 0	0 4 2	0 17 6	0 10 0

Glasnevin Cemetery, c. 1910. Daniel O'Connell was instrumental in the setting up of Prospect, later Glasnevin, Cemetery. It was established in 1832 as a Catholic burial ground, but with the stipulation that plots could be provided for those of different faiths. Since its establishment it has become the final resting place for over one million people, some famous, some infamous.

The iconic O'Connell Monument, seen in the top left image, was in the style of the round towers of medieval Christian Ireland. The tower was constructed to mark the tomb of Daniel O'Connell, who passed away in Genoa in 1847. While his body was repatriated, his heart, as per his wishes, was buried in Rome. The tower was completed in 1869 and has been bombed twice – once in 1952, the victim of a bored schoolboy up to no good, and more seriously in 1971, when northern loyalists bombed it and several other symbols of republican Ireland.
(*Courtesy of the Glasnevin Trust*)

The Casino, Marino. This area was originally part of the estate of the Earls of Charlemont and was developed for housing in the 1920s and 1930s. This neoclassical pavilion, commissioned by the 1st Earl and finished in the 1770s, is the only part of the estate that survives. A disused tunnel under the Casino was used by Michael Collins and others to practise firing Thompson sub-machine guns which had been purchased for the IRA in America. (*Courtesy of the National Library of Ireland*)

INDEX